SHAKARDOKHT JAFARI was born in Daykundi, Afghanistan in 1977 and grew up as a refugee in Iran, where she completed her BSc in radiation technologies at Tabriz University of Medical Sciences. After moving back to Afghanistan, she secured a teaching post in radiology at Kabul Medical University. In 2010 she moved to the University of Surrey in the UK to study a master's in medical physics, becoming the first Afghanistani woman to earn a PhD in that subject. She was awarded the Schlumberger Foundation Faculty for the Future award for her second year of studies. The founder of her own radiation technology company, she is a winner of a Women in Innovation award and is chair of Education Bridge for Afghanistan.

'A fascinating journey from rural Afghanistan to the world of research and academia in rural England. The juxtaposition of the personal and the political makes this an enticingly interesting read'
Baroness Warsi, former Foreign Office minister

'Shakardokht Jafari's journey from war to medicine will inspire many. This is a wonderful book and a darned good read that ultimately makes us all want to do better'
Deborah Ellis, author of *The Breadwinner*

'A deeply emotional and inspiring book that will stay with you long after you turn the last page. A must-read for anyone interested in the history, culture, and politics of Afghanistan, and a timely reminder of the resilience and strength of Afghan women'
Waseem Mahmood, author of *Good Morning Afghanistan*

Shakar

Shakar

A Woman's Journey from Afghanistan

Shakardokht Jafari

EYE BOOKS

Published by Eye Books
29A Barrow Street
Much Wenlock
Shropshire
TF13 6EN

www.eye-books.com

Cover design by Ifan Bates
Typeset in Baskerville

British Library Cataloguing in Publication Data
A catalogue record for this book is available from the British Library

ISBN 9781785633553

Contents

Prologue

APRIL 2019. LONDON Heathrow Airport, Terminal 5, arrivals side. We trundle our hand luggage along the interminable corridors, always following the signs to UK Border Controls: Passports, then look for the channel for All Other Passports. The queue is not huge but there is no sign of movement – not surprising given that more than half the passport control booths are unmanned. Passengers are mostly quiet and expressionless, resigned to the lengthy process, the dull wait before the stressful double-checking of documents and the banality of the repeated questions.

As we step into the maze of barriers policing the lines of the queues, a uniformed official approaches us. Perhaps she has spotted our blue and gold Afghan passports. She asks us a few questions, and we explain our circumstances. Her expression changes, and she requests us to follow her to a priority queue.

'You should expect to get through in about 45 minutes', she smiles. Was there a faint hint of apology in that smile? I wonder.

Ibrahim touches me gently on the arm.

'Are you sure you're going to be OK?'

'Yes, I think I can stand for that long.'

He is concerned because I am eight months pregnant, and in an ideal world wouldn't be risking air travel. But I had set my heart on attending the conference in Milan. My project – *the* project – had been ready for its international launch, and I knew that everyone who was anyone would be at the annual symposium of the European Society of Radiotherapy and Oncology. To be honest, even now I'm glowing from the impact of the presentation; the attention and encouragement it attracted from the other delegates; the media coverage.

But pregnancy was not the only jeopardy in my travelling abroad. I had been diagnosed several months earlier with breast cancer. At one point it looked inevitable that the pregnancy would have to be terminated, but miraculously a way of saving the baby's life had been found. Even so, I have had surgery, and flew out in the interval of a course of chemotherapy. We had gone knowing full well that I was likely to give birth early, because of the hormone imbalances in the body from the illness and its treatment. So the trip to Italy had been…I don't like to say 'a gamble', but I'm not sure what else you could call it. I remember while we were in Italy saying, over and over, to the little creature inside me: 'Please, don't be born here!'

And now I'm so happy that my voice was heard.

We are approaching the head of the queue when Ibrahim touches my arm again. He points up at the huge video display above the passport booths. I glance up, and have the surreal experience of seeing myself looking back at me from the screen. The video presentation is promoting the UK as a welcoming place for researchers and innovators, and here I am, an Afghanistani woman, telling the world how my discovery in the field of radiation science led to me winning the Women in Innovation UK Award.

At that moment we are called forward to passport control. The immigration officer flicks through my passport and asks what I do for a living. 'Clinical scientist,' I tell him. 'Oh, and innovator, too. Look. That's me up there   that's my video showing above your head!'

He looks up, looks back at me, smiles briefly, and reaches for his official stamp. I have never got through passport control so quickly in my life.

1

This is my *watan*

I'M STANDING ON THE EDGE of our village, looking out and away. Shouldering the skyline are the mountains: arid, donkey-coloured, monumental, and for all I know repeating to the ends of the earth. Below, nearer to hand, are the fields where my father and uncles work. A river runs between the fields, and closer to where I stand, down the slope, by the side of the river there is a tree. And in the tree, I can see a woodpecker. I am, I would guess, four or five years old.

It's strange, what our minds choose to remember. There's nothing especially significant in this postcard from the past, but of the many hundreds and thousands of possible memories from my childhood, this is one that comes back to me. Why? It is neither typical nor atypical, and I cannot read any symbolism into the tree, or the woodpecker. But it might, perhaps, represent a moment, a turning point, in my growing up. Nobody told me to look at the woodpecker in the tree. Nobody else saw it. It was a strangely personal moment – my secret – and so perhaps I locked it away in a special place in my mind, a place to treasure those things I alone knew: my discoveries.

If the woodpecker had flown away (which I don't remember), or I had given up watching it, and had turned around, I would have had pretty much the whole of our village in sight. Aral, the only place I had known in my short life, was a settlement of about twenty households, situated roughly halfway between Kabul and Herat, in the mountainous Bandar & Sang Takht region of Afghanistan's central Daykundi province. The houses in Aral were traditional Afghan mud houses, with walls of clay mixed with straw, reinforced with a framework of wood. The walls, especially those in guest rooms, were sometimes painted, using coloured stone crushed into powder and mixed into an emulsion. Ceilings were spans of horizontal wooden poles, finished above with mud and straw to make flat roofs, where crops or fabric could be laid out to dry.

Ours was a farming community, and one of the most important rooms in the house was for the animals: cows, sheep, goats and chickens. Everybody also kept dogs, but they were not allowed in the home. The animal room connected to the living space with a fireplace in the middle of the house. There was a hole in the roof to let out smoke, with a cover that could be removed in summer for ventilation. Fuel was not easy to come by. We used to go out gathering brushwood, and in summer people would collect animal dung and dry it in the sun to burn on the fire in the winter.

The main room in the house – the living room – had no sofas, but in the evenings we would sit on big sturdy cushions set against the wall. The whole household slept here, too, or in the guest room, on futons. There were always plenty of spare futons, in case we had guests. In the daytime they were piled in one corner, to keep the room tidy. The guest room was the most elaborately decorated room in the house, with big curtains and embroidery made by the women.

As a little girl, I used to spend a lot of time with my mum, watching her at her tasks and learning to help out. Like all Afghan women, my mother worked a long, hard day, filled with routines. The household would wake before sunrise, when the adults took prayers, then Mum would make sure the fire in the bread oven in the kitchen was lit, and mix some dough. Next, to milk the cow, and the sheep and goats. Back to the kitchen to bake the bread, then prepare a simple breakfast of sweetened tea and the warm bread from the oven. By now it was time to send the animals out to graze on the mountains. This was a job often entrusted to children, and became one of my responsibilities when I was as young as four or five years old. While I was herding the animals up the hill, I'd watch the men heading out to work, to tend the crops in the fields.

Meanwhile, with everyone out of the house, Mum would get on with cleaning and sweeping the floors. Her next task was to go down to the meadow to collect fodder for the animals. This was *shaftal*, or Persian clover, a nutritious crop that we cultivated for the purpose. It could be eaten fresh, or batches would be spread on the roof to dry, and be stored as a winter feed. There were other plants that we foraged in spring and summer to be dried for winter fodder, and I remember *gheghu*, a perennial related to fennel, and *kamai*, one of the prangos family, with its starbursts of tiny yellow flowers.

As for our own human diet, one of the staples was yoghurt. Before lunch, Mum would boil some of the milk she'd drawn earlier in the day, for tomorrow's yoghurt. Yesterday's boiled milk would have been hung from a tripod in a *mashq*, or goatskin bag, and shaken to separate out the butter. What was left was a watery yoghurt, which we would have for lunch, soaked into hunks of Mum's fresh bread that we'd dip into our bowls. The surplus would be boiled up to thicken and dry into *quroot*, a cheese-like savoury that Mum preserved with salt to keep for winter.

Meals would be from staple ingredients: the yoghurt and butter, grain flour cooked in various ways, and potatoes. Often, we would have a porridge of boiled wheat, which Mum served with fresh yoghurt blended into a sauce with onion, mint and garlic. Alternatively, she might make corn porridge, served with butter, or we would have corn bread. We had rice too, but this was usually reserved for special occasions. If the men of the house were working nearby, they would come home for lunch; otherwise one of us children would be sent to take the lunch out to them in the fields.

Some of the morning's routines would be repeated after lunch: milking the animals, and baking fresh bread for dinner. Otherwise, Mum's afternoons were devoted to handiwork, such as weaving thread into rugs, making wool, or repairing our clothes. Then a short evening: dinner, after which the men would go to bed, while the women might stay up to do more needlework by lamplight. There was no electricity; no gas. No running water, either: water was collected from the spring, which all the villagers shared. They had built a shed over it, where we would go to bathe, and where Mum would wash our clothes and dishes. As for any basic essentials we were unable to make ourselves, such as soap, sugar, or oil for the lanterns, a trip had to be made to the nearest town. Aral was too small to support a proper store, although we did have a tiny shop, which I remember sold little notebooks made from cut-up packing material. Paper was such a scarce resource, and these tiny books made me appreciate its value. Even now I never throw paper away, and always make full use of both sides.

That was the summer season. In our climate, the period from late autumn until early spring was not so much winter as 'snow season'. There was so much snow, we could do nothing outside. Snow would pile up, two metres high, and men would shovel alleyways between the houses, the snow walls too high even for adults to see over. And it brought the further problem that because the weight of so much snow was more than our flat roofs were built to bear, it had to be frequently swept or shovelled from them to prevent collapse.

The roads (dirt tracks; no tarmac) were blocked by snow, so there was no access to the doctor. This was a dangerous time to be ill. When I was nine months old, there was an outbreak of measles in Aral. With no medication, nearly all the children died. All except two: one was my cousin, who survived because he had immunity from birth. I didn't have immunity, and went into a coma. I wasn't expected to survive. What saved me I don't know, but somehow, my parents' prayers were answered. After three days, I regained consciousness.

In winter, with fewer farming chores, we had more time

on our hands. From the age of six or seven, children were expected to study. There were no professional teachers, no means of funding education at a local level, so the teachers were educated men from the village. My father was one of these, and because of this I think I may have started learning at an earlier age. I remember Dad making a drawing of the alphabet using flowers, to help us in learning to read. Lessons in reading and writing were held in the village hall, where there were a few books: essentially of course the Qur'an, some novels, and a book I remember from childhood, the Persian *Shāh-nāmeh* (Book of Kings) epic poem.

The village hall was also where decisions were made on behalf of the villagers. Women didn't have much say in this. Village leadership was hereditary, and it was the task of the *darughah* or *kadkhoda* – the leaders – to quell violence and resolve disputes. This would be done locally wherever possible, or failing that, the dispute would be taken to the seats of regional or central government where the leaders had a voice. Much power and influence also rested with the *khans*, who were equivalent perhaps of the aristocracy in England: the richest members of the community, landowners and employers, with the authority to pass judgements. This system was quite autocratic, with no right of appeal against the khans. The individual power they enjoyed in office extended into their personal lives, sometimes to the detriment of others. For example, if one of the khans or leaders wanted a girl for themselves, or for one of their sons, nobody else would be allowed to marry that girl. She would be given no choice.

It was very much a society bound by rules, and the rules always promoted family over the individual. Marriages were mostly arranged, but now and again you would hear of boys and girls meeting in the fields, or up in the mountains when shepherding the animals. If they wanted a relationship that they knew would not be condoned by their families, sometimes they would take a romantic but drastic course: escaping, and running off together. Whenever this happened, the girl would not be allowed back into the family, and the boy's family would have to negotiate reparation with the family of the girl. In any marriage, the boy's family always has to pay, not only for the ceremony but also for whatever goods and chattels are needed for the couple to set up home. So the parents of any boy are always extra vigilant regarding relationships.

In between working and obeying rules, we still managed to find time for fun, especially when there was something to celebrate. Folk music was a part of any ceremony, sung and played on a long flute called the *ney*, and on a slender two-stringed lute, the *dutar* or *dambura*. The musicianship was good, and we even had a famous musician raised in our neighbouring village – Dawood Sarkhosh, who now has an international career as a singer and player of the *dambura*. Women would recite poetry, while for the men this was a great excuse for making plenty of noise with gunfire, as guns were widespread for hunting and protection. Social gatherings also often featured competitions to hit targets, and wrestling bouts, mostly for boys. There was no alcohol, but it was permitted to use tobacco – which people planted and grew themselves – dried and powdered and made into a moist paste called *nās*, held in the mouth under the lip or in the cheek.

Such was our family's day-to-day life, similar to the lives of so many in our country's farming communities. But when it comes to describing the social, ethnic and religious structures that are so important in Afghanistan, I need to step back a little, to the time of the earlier generations of our family. Because many years before I was born, something happened that had the most profound consequences on my life, and the lives of all of my family.

Our country has two major religious groups: Sunni and Shia, whose irreconcilable division is seen as lying at the heart of the nation's troubles. In Afghanistan, religion is paramount. Praying is paramount. Aral is a Shia village, so the villagers must pray three times a day. This is one of the distinctions from the Sunnis, who pray five times a day. Shias combine the lunchtime and afternoon prayer times of the Sunnis into one, likewise the sunset and evening prayers. The religious calendar includes a month of fasting, when girls from the age of nine would fast and pray. Boys would not begin to do this until the age of fourteen or fifteen. I remember struggling with having to fast as a nine-year-old, in the long days of summer, when the hunger was intense and I would have to lie down in the afternoons, drained of energy. Religious observance was obligatory, of course, and it would never have crossed my mind to rebel. Anyone who did not practise would be ostracised, at the very least. They might even be killed.

So, given the rift between the two religious practices, it may appear surprising, unlikely even, that my great-grandparents were one of each persuasion: he was Sunni, while she was Shia. Their unusual marriage came about because in the

1920s there was a drought in the village and local area, at a time when neighbouring provinces had a surplus of crops. This opened up a very particular trading opportunity that was seen to be a good thing in a country of scattered communities: people from the outlying area came to Aral to barter crops in exchange for girls to be taken as brides. One of those girls was my great-grandmother, who was given to one of the visiting sons in marriage. She was Shia, and of Hazara ethnicity, while he was Sunni and Aimagh. It was allowed (as I'm not sure it would be allowed today) that each kept their own religion. My great-grandmother was taken to the village of her husband, whose name was Malik Momeni. The couple went on to have three children, before Malik was unexpectedly taken ill and died, still, I think, in his twenties. The eldest child, a boy, was then only six or seven years old; there was a daughter, aged four, and a second son aged two.

Usually in this situation (which was not so infrequent, in a country with such high mortality rates) a brother of the dead husband would be obliged to offer to marry the widow, when necessary as his second wife. But my great-grandmother did not want that. She returned to her home village to live with her brothers, even though, in accordance with traditional law, that meant leaving the children behind to be cared for by the father's family.

But the eldest son, Khair Mohammad Momeni, escaped and travelled alone from his father's village to his mother's, which for an adult would be two or three days' walking. I've no idea how he survived, or found his way. The uncles, his father's brothers, came to his mother's village, 'collected' him (perhaps 'kidnapped' would be closer to the truth) and took him back. But Khair ran away to his mother again, and this time when the uncles arrived, all the villagers stood up against them. The uncles were told that it was best for the son to remain where he wanted to be, with his mother. At the same time they were warned not to return again. If they did, they should expect a fight.

So Khair stayed in the village with his mother. The spirit he had shown in leaving his father's village, his strong sense of independence and determination, stayed with him as he threw himself into learning, studying literacy with the Mullah, and going on to visit Iran and Iraq for religious education. He changed his religion from his father's, the religion he would normally inherit, to his mother's, and in due course became religious leader of the village. He changed his family name, too, from the Sunni name of his father, Momeni, to his mother's Shia name: Jafari.

Khair Mohammad Jafari was my grandfather. He married, and became a children's teacher. This had the disadvantage that he became poor, as he was unable to work in the fields. He became father to seven children, four boys and three girls. One boy and one girl died in childhood; of the remaining boys, Mirza Ali Jafari was my father. When they were old enough, my father and his brothers were sent out to work, rather than go to school, so that the family would have some income. But my father was precocious, with a bright intelligence and hunger to learn, so he took lessons early in the morning before work, and again when he came home in the evening. The value of education became a cornerstone of his life, and he went on to become an expert in religious studies.

Meanwhile, my father's eldest brother, Mohammad Ali, had been promised to a girl but did not have the money to start the marriage, so it was agreed that he should work first for the girl's father for a couple of years until he could afford to pay. But when the physical side of the relationship developed too far, too soon, against the rules, my uncle was thrown out. Not only that, but my father, who had done nothing wrong, was then obliged to perform my uncle's work duties, to compensate for his absence. He worked in this way for Haji Ghulam for two years, before being conscripted into the army, as all young men were.

Thanks to his father's teaching, he was one of the very few recruits with numeracy and literacy skills, and so was assigned to special duties. During the Cold War, both America and the Soviet Union had kept a toehold in the country by funding and overseeing infrastructure projects. These included hydro-electric dams, bridges, public buildings such as universities, and highways. My father was tasked with working alongside Soviet engineers on improving the road structure. When the two-year term of conscription ended, he would normally have graduated and returned home. But the army had nobody to replace him in his job, so he was compelled to stay on in the military, based in Kabul and working across the country in Mazar-e-Sharif, Kandahar and Herat. Mirza Ali Jafari went on to serve ten years, becoming very knowledgeable about highway engineering.

When my father had holiday time, he used to return to the village, where his brother Mohammad Ali was by now reconciled with his parents. On one visit Dad asked his brother's wife, Hawasil, if her younger sister, Narma, was still alive. He remembered her from the times he was working in the fields, when as a girl she used to bring him his lunch. Now, he thought, she would be grown up, and would make a good wife. She was then living with an uncle and aunt in a neighbouring village, so my father went to meet her there and an engagement was arranged. But on a subsequent visit to the village, he was told by one of the neighbours that the aunt and uncle were abusive towards his fiancée. He tried to persuade her to return with him to Kabul, where he worked, but she was frightened off the idea by Hawasil and by the uncle and aunt. So my father quit his army job to return to the village, get married, set up home with my mum, and work in the fields.

And so we arrive at the day when I entered the world: 8 August, 1977. The very fact that I know my precise date of birth is unusual, because birthdays didn't matter to us very much and were often forgotten. But I can say for sure which day it was, because my father wrote the dates and times of his children's births down in his Qur'an. My birth is recorded in my father's hand by the date according to the Shamsi Hijri calendar, the principal calendar of Afghanistan: '18/05/1356'.

My name, Shakardokht, is unusual too, and has – literally – a story behind it. My birth affected my uncle, Mohammad Ali, deeply. My father and uncle were both then living in what had been the house of their parents, who had by this time passed away. My uncle had two sons, Mohammad Hussein, who was sixteen, and Mohammad Hassan, aged twelve. There had been a daughter born between the two boys, and she had died very young. So when I was born, my uncle saw me as a gift to fill the place of his lost daughter. He insisted on the right to name me, and chose my name from a Sanskrit epic poem he happened to be reading at the time, *Wameq and Uzra* by Moeinuddin Peshawari. Shakardokht, meaning 'sweet girl', was the name of a fictional princess of China, who was a heroine in the book. I still remember some lines from the poem, that my father and uncle used to read to me:

> *This is the Shakardokht that people are talking about,*
> *Shakardokht is the daughter of the fagfur* (emperor) *of China.*

All I have written about my *watan* – my homeland – and the way of life of its inhabitants may have given the impression that nothing much had changed for scores of years, even for centuries. There are two obvious reasons why this might be: in our country we adhere to social and religious strictures that promote a deep conservatism, an innate sense of duty to tradition; and we are a very poor country, in a world where progress is bought.

But that is not to say that in Afghanistan there was no hunger for change. And while I was still a baby, the changes had already begun.

2

Farewell, Roqaya

JUST ONE YEAR AFTER my birth, there was an uprising in Afghanistan, aiming for modernisation and land reform. This followed the Saur (April) Revolution, a socialist coup that established a democratic republic. It was repressive and brutal, leading to the deaths of many opponents, and it was supported by the Soviet Union. There was a backlash – a rebellion – with armed militias being raised across the country, especially in rural areas. These were the Mujahideen, literally 'those engaged in jihad'. They soon won the backing of the United States, Pakistan, Iran, Saudi Arabia, China, and the United Kingdom, in what became a nine-year-long guerrilla conflict (the Soviet-Afghan War) against the Democratic Republic and their backers, the Soviet Army, which invaded the country at the end of 1979.

However much we opposed the war, and the threat it posed to the survival of rural communities such as ours, we could not evade it. In Afghanistan, the opinions and allegiances of the individual counted for nothing against the markers of religion, sect and ethnicity. Because the Shia religious leaders were among the Mujahideen, there was a lot of prejudice against Shia people generally. In the case of our particular family, things were complicated further by the historic marriage of Sunni and Shia bloodlines.

Add into the mix our Hazara ethnicity, and we suddenly found ourselves with many enemies in our own community. Hazaras are an Afghan minority group whose homeland is the mountainous Hazarajat central region of the country, in which Daykundi is situated. We were once thought to be in part genetically Mongol, but studies on the shape of Buddha statues in Hazarajat, which pre-date the Mongol invasion, suggest that Hazaras are actually indigenous. Culturally, and in physical appearance, we have maintained an autonomy from the Pashtuns, the politically dominant group in Afghanistan. Consisting of several hundred tribes and clans, the Pashtuns consider themselves aboriginal Afghans; in fact in certain contexts the term 'Afghan' is reserved exclusively for Pahstuns, with the country's other ethnicities – people like me – labelled 'Afghanistani'. The Pashtun diaspora includes Pakistan and northern India, and to a lesser extent Iran. In Afghanistan they are the ruling ethnic group, whose control of the country and protection of their own status has led at times to prejudice against – and sometimes persecution of – ethnic minorities, including the Hazaras.

Before I had reached the age of six, the internal conflict in Afghanistan had become intolerable. It was especially dangerous for my father who, because of his religion and ethnicity, was branded as a member of a fighting group. His education, and even his own father's religious learning, made things worse, labelling him a Mullah and, by association, an enemy of the government. In their eyes, and in the eyes of the khans who were their influential supporters at a local level, we were lumped in with the guerrillas and the Mujahideen, many of whom were − like us − Persian-speaking Shiite Hazaras.

We were guilty by association, too, with our neighbour state, Iran, which had come out in support of the Shia Mujahideen. Iran had only a few years before, at the end of the 1970s, seen a revolution of its own, with the deposition of the Shah and the establishment of the world's first Islamic Republic under Ayatollah Khomeini, the appointed Supreme Leader.

There was even division among the Hazara people, represented by no fewer than eight principal political parties. They would later unite, but at this time three of those parties held power locally: Sazman-e Nasr was the Victory Organisation, consisting mainly of educated people, such as my father and uncle, who were supporting enlightenment. The Pasdaran organisation had similar aims to Nasr, while in our area the third party, Shura-i Engelab, was constituted of big land owners.

When fighting broke out between Shura-i Engelab on the one side, and Nasr and Pasdaran on the other, my father was fearful of getting killed by the Shura. He left the village with my uncle, and with the uncle's younger son − those who were most at risk. They fled up into the mountains, and hid out in a cave for more than two months. Even in that remote place, they witnessed fighting at first hand. This was a wake-up call, resolving them to make urgent plans for the family to flee, while we still could.

As luck would have it, my mother was in contact with somebody who was able to secure (with, I suspect, some money changing hands) an official letter of safe conduct from the head of Shura-i Engelab, to take the family out of the village and start their journey. This was, in a way, our passport to freedom.

When my father returned home, my parents sold what they could of their house, furniture and other possessions, and some animals. Villagers were upset that we were leaving, abandoning the village, as it seemed to them. There were so many families planning to flee that those intending to remain put obstacles in our path. So my parents let it be known that they were going to live and work for a year or so in another village, Dane Khairali, with my mother's father. My father travelled there and met a friend, Mirza Hussain, an educated religious leader who also wanted to travel to Iran. In the past he had sometimes come to our village to buy wheat, and now he came to our rescue. My father brought him back to Aral with his two horses. Mum, who was then pregnant, sat on one, while the other was loaded with wheat, and I sat on top of the wheat. My four-year-old brother, Mohammad Baqer, and my little one-year-old sister, Roqaya, were scooped up, and so we left our village.

We came to a river that we had to cross. Mirza Hussain was not familiar with the river, or where best to cross. When he found what he thought was a good place, my horse did not want to wade in. Mirza pushed from behind and reluctantly the horse went in. But the river was deep, too deep for the horse, and a sudden surge toppled us. I was thrown from my perch, and both Mirza and the horse were swept into the water. There was a danger we might all be washed away. Luckily, Mirza was able to swim, strongly enough to come to my rescue, pulling me to safety. The horse, meanwhile, floated down to a shallower part of the river and regained the river bank about a hundred metres downstream. When I looked round, I saw that most of the rest of our party were standing on the bank, watching helplessly, because none of them knew how to swim. Without Mirza's help, I'm sure I would have drowned. I had to strip my wet clothes off and Mum draped them over the back of a cow to dry, while I was wrapped in some cloth to keep me warm.

When we reached my grandfather's house, there was a warm welcome, and a lot of fuss was made over us children. But the journey had hardly begun, and we were straightaway busied with preparations. Cuts of meat were fried in oil until they started to become hard and dry, and then packed with plenty of salt as preservative. We made cookies too, called *bosuragh*, of wheat flour with a little sugar and salt, again fried to dryness to last on the journey. The group of us who were travelling together gradually assembled, which took a long time, largely because of the difficulties some had in selling farm animals and household possessions. We took these things to a nearby village, to sell at market. Finally, it was time to go. I remember how sad I was saying goodbye to my grandfather, a wonderful and wise man, sitting quietly in his chair in his large house.

It was in the spring of 1983, while I was still five years old, that we set off. We had horses, and three donkeys. Mum rode on one donkey, we kids were on a second (tied on with rope, as we didn't know how to ride a donkey), and the third in the line carried food and bedding. The men walked, and the convoy was completed with the animals that we were unable to sell, which we brought with us to slaughter and eat on the way.

Our group was my immediate family, as well as my uncle and cousins. We were part of a greater trek, of something like 1,200 households from the interior of the country, heading south and west towards the border which was five hundred or more miles distant. What drove us was the threat of the men being made to join fighting groups. We had heard that Iran, sympathetic to our plight, had opened its borders. 'Islam has no border', was our rallying cry.

Along the way there was a lot of bombing. The Soviet-Afghan war was being fought in the mountains: the targets were not strategic but human, so the fighting continued wherever people could go, even into the most hostile terrain. Refugees were classed as anti-government, of course, so we were a target. One girl I knew was killed by a bomb. Many others – children and the elderly in particular – died on the road. Anyone who died was buried straightaway in a makeshift grave, and it was grievous for a family to leave one of its own out there, in that loveless nowhere. Sometimes, it was too dangerous to stop even to dig a grave, and I remember when one boy lost his mum, the group allowed him only to cover her body with a chador, weighed down with stones on the corners, before pulling him away so that we could continue the journey.

Each day we would start out very early, before it got too hot. We would trek until mid to late morning, when travel became impossible, the heat too intense for us and our poor pack animals. We would take a few hours' shelter, and share some food, then move off again in the late afternoon, walking into the sunset. Then we'd set up a makeshift camp, tend to the animals, eat, and finally sleep, on a duvet on the open ground, our whole family on a single duvet.

Slowly, a few miles at a time, we made our way out of our province, Daykundi, and across the northern reaches of Helmand. We kept off the main thoroughfares, following herdsmen's tracks and local roads. The terrain was rugged, switching from rocky mountain passes, through a patchwork scrubland of poor vegetation and bare grey soil, to expanses of desert. Everywhere was dry and dusty. I remember a few moments of relief, such as when we were in one of the areas near a town, and for the first time ever we saw a bicycle and a tractor. Everybody ran to watch these absurd contraptions, which were so funny to look at.

After several months, we entered Nimroz province, in the south-west of our country. This was the final province for most refugees, before crossing either into Iran, or Pakistan. Near the town of Bakwa we found a school building, with only the walls standing, which is where we stayed for one month, to recoup our strength and await the opening of the Iran border. The journey had been hard and the food insufficient. Sometimes on the way we had begged bread from gypsies, or else young men from our group offered to work for the gypsies in exchange for food. In Nimroz, we improvised as well as we could for money or food. For instance, some of the lakes and swamps in this region are salty, from minerals washed down from the mountains, and my father made salt, which he then sold or bartered, by boiling the salty water. Young people went to neighbouring villages, to work for bread and watermelons. At one time the river flooded, and there was a glut of stranded fish, but most of our party had no experience of fish and didn't know how to cook them.

There was a lot of bad water, and consequently a lot of illness. Some of the older people died of bad water. My eighteen-month-old sister Roqaya contracted diarrhoea. She couldn't eat ordinary bread, and would beg for watermelon. We had no doctor with us, nobody with training in healthcare, and we relied on folk wisdom for remedies. According to that folk wisdom, watermelon was bad for patients with diarrhoea, so it was refused my sister. Later, much too late, we learned that it would have been good for her. But the poor little creature wasted away, and died, and was buried, at that school in Nimroz. It seemed so unfair, for somebody so young. Another innocent victim of…so very many unnecessary things.

We left the school, six months into the trip, knowing now that our destination was Iran. Not all of us: some of the larger group had already left for Pakistan, leaving a convoy of around 1,000. But we had one final obstacle, in the form of Hamun Lake, a vast shallow expanse of water with surrounding wetlands, all fed by the thawing of the mountain snows in spring. The lake was officially closed, but traffickers were at work, and there were bamboo boats called *tuteen* to hire. Help came also from Iranian border control guards, who allowed refugees to stay on an island in the lake until granted permission to enter Iran.

But now, at this final stage, the cooperation that had sustained us in the journey turned to competition to get over the border: tempers flared, and fighting broke out, with people weeping. I remember my aunt pinching my leg to make me cry, in the hope that the sight of a little girl in tears might attract sympathy.

Somehow, in the chaos, we got permission to cross the border, and suddenly found ourselves at the start of our new lives: refugees in Iran. There was a sense of a burden being lifted. We knew at last that we were saved from the pressing dangers that had driven us to make this perilous journey; we gave thanks for our survival, and prayed for those we had lost on the way.

But what exactly had we gained? As refugees, our future was a blank, our prospects – of work and income for my parents, of education for us children – less certain than ever. Whatever might happen next was out of our hands. Any decisions would be made for us, by the immigration officials, and by the military. All we could do was hope, and pray, and obey orders.

3

One family, one spoon

OUR FAMILY GROUP MAKING the crossing had been just one small part of a huge exodus which, during the 1980s, saw one Afghan citizen in about every five leaving their homeland, bound for either Iran or Pakistan. The Iranian government was maintaining an open-door policy at the time we arrived in the country, but the situation was volatile, and there would come a flashpoint when refugee numbers came to be seen as a problem. For now, one of the main concerns of the Iranian government appeared to be the avoidance of any concentration of Afghan refugee populations. So while families were kept together, the larger group we had travelled with was divided and dispersed to various towns and villages.

We had crossed the border into Iran's south-easterly province of Beluchistan, where we were initially given shelter by kindly local villagers. After a few days, our family was moved on to the province's capital, Zabol, a small city with a population of around 130,000. A substantial minority of the city's inhabitants are Sistani Persians, who are Shia and whose dialect is very similar to our Farsi. And although this was a much larger community than we were used to, the way of life here was not so different from back home, with similar habits and rituals, such as baking bread in a clay oven at home every morning. This made it much easier for us to fit in, and we found the local people compassionate and generous in their hospitality. Here was the warm welcome we had prayed for.

And there was another welcome in store. My mum had been pregnant during our journey, and a month or two after we arrived in Zabol she gave birth to a baby girl. In token of our safe passage into the country, my parents named her Masumeh, after the Muslim saint of Iranian birth. Fatima Masumeh was the sister of the eighth, and daughter of the seventh, of the Twelve Imams, the disciples of Mohammed. Her brother is buried at the Imam Reza Shrine in Iran's second-largest city, Mashhad, while the vast and significant Hazrat Fatima Masumeh Holy Shrine is in the sacred city of Qom, outside Tehran.

Masumeh was just three days old when the Iranian government announced that refugees from Afghanistan would be given a choice. Either we could settle in a camp under the provision of the UN High Commissioner for Refugees (UNHCR), with the guarantee of food and shelter but no immediate prospects. Or, we could choose to find work, without support, and integrate into the community. The first option had its appeal for some of the elderly and less capable, those who would welcome the assistance and surety of having their basic needs met. But my father could see that our best future would come from him committing to find work and care for the family, away from any camp.

Prospects were poor in Zabol, and we wanted to avoid the season of the notorious '120-day wind', a cloying dust storm which makes this one of the world's most polluted cities. My uncle was keen that we should all go to Mashhad, where his son, who had travelled to Iran one year earlier, was now living. This is a city ten hours' drive to the north of Zabol, close to the border with Turkmenistan. But in determining how refugees would be distributed nationally, the government had ruled out Mashhad and Tehran. Instead, my father and uncle were told they should go to the city of Isfahan, in Iran's interior, and were issued with the appropriate travel warrants and documents for us all. We actually got as far as the bus terminal, where transport would be waiting for us, when by chance my father bumped into a distant relation who had been living in Iran for a few years. When my dad explained our predicament, the man offered to have a word with the bus driver. 'Think how much quicker, and cheaper for you, it would be to take these people to Mashhad, rather than all the way to Isfahan?' he told the bus driver. 'And don't worry', he went on, 'if they question you at any checkpoint, on why you are not taking them to Isfahan. All you have to do is explain how important it would be for these new arrivals in our country to visit the holy shrine at Mashhad.' Luckily, the bus driver was persuaded, and we all – our family and my uncle's family – boarded the bus.

It was the start of the winter season, towards the end of 1983, when we arrived in Mashhad. My father and his brother were told that if they wanted to pick up work, the best place to go was Ab Square, the bustling central piazza, where every kind of transaction was carried out, including the hiring of casual labour. Each morning, they would negotiate wages with one of the *sar-amale*, the hiring foremen, and the piecework they picked up earned them enough to meet the cost of bread and basic provisions. In the square, another chance encounter with an old friend led to us all being offered temporary accommodation in one room.

On days when they had no success in finding employment in the square, my dad and uncle began the search for my cousin. It took about three months to find him, working on a farm away from the city centre. Once he joined us, the elders of the family debated our best next move. It was determined – no doubt my uncle, as family elder, would have had the final say – that we would all travel to Tehran.

My dad hadn't brought his road construction qualifications with him from Afghanistan, so began looking instead to make use of the skills he'd acquired working in the fields. He received a message from a distant relation, the father of the wife of one of my cousins. They had travelled to Iran one year earlier, and he was now employed at a market garden in Tehran. When he heard about us being in Mashhad, he let Dad know that there was a vacancy for another worker in the garden, and asked if he would be interested. Meanwhile my uncle, with his sons and daughter-in-law, found work on a farm which was also outside Tehran, where they would be about an hour's journey from us. So with spring coming, we all left Mashhad, and took the bus to Tehran.

We found our new home in Khatoon Abad town, at a garden in a large walled enclosure where flowers – Iran is famous for its roses – and some fruit were cultivated. It lay in the outer suburbs of Tehran, fourteen kilometres from the city centre, situated close to the town of Pakdasht. This was our new home, and how different it was from our old one in Aral! Instead of mountains, we looked out across a flat dusty plain. Instead of mud houses, most of the buildings were brick and concrete and steel. And instead of horses and donkeys, there was an endless stream of cars and lorries and pickup trucks and mopeds, thundering close to the wall of the garden along one of the main arterial roads into the city, the Imam Reza highway. It may not have been picturesque, but I found all this new energy was exciting.

First, we met the owner. He was known as Haji Hussein Damaghani, as one who had been on the hajj, the pilgrimage to Mecca that every Muslim is meant to do at least once in their life, but we children learned to call him Baba Haji. He and his wife lived in the garden, in a house modern enough to be built of brick, with oil central heating. Six of their children were married, with another two still living at home. Baba Haji was in his 60s, white-haired, not particularly educated or literate, but very religious. He and my father both followed the same religious rules, and soon they were best buddies, endlessly discussing religious matters over work. He nicknamed my father 'Mashti Mullah': Mashti was a name given to one who had visited the shrine at Mashhad, while Mullah was simply someone with religious knowledge.

They allocated us accommodation in one corner of the garden, in what looked like a throwback to one of the houses back home, with those familiar walls of clay mixed with straw, and a roof of wooden poles. There was one room, with an annexe which we used as a kitchen-cum-utility room. Next door was a byre, which held six or seven cows. But the most vivid of all my recollections of that place is the mulberry tree outside our house, a big tree that we used to climb to go onto the roof. To us children, that somehow made it ours, our own exclusive territory. Ever since, I have thought mulberries are the best of all fruit. In fact, I still dream of picking mulberries from that lovely tree.

I remember from our early days in the garden that when we ate dinner, we all had to share one spoon. We had been able to bring so little with us, and my father was earning only enough for the most basic requirements. Gradually, one piece at a time, we acquired more necessities: a dish and a bowl, more spoons, a length of carpet. The carpet served as a bed for all of us, in place of a mattress or duvet. We lay in a line along one side of the carpet, and if it was cold, pulled the other half on top of us.

While my dad was working on the garden, Mum took on responsibility for tending the cows. She was paid one day's milk every week in exchange, which she used to make butter and yoghurt, just as she had in Afghanistan. She sold any excess milk to the neighbours. I sometimes silently wished she might have sold more of it, because she served us yoghurt mixed with breadcrumbs for breakfast so often that I grew to hate it. Even now, I flinch from having to eat it again. As we had so little money, our main meals were simple dishes such as a potato and onion stew, or bread with gravy. Meat – chicken or lamb – was a luxury, that we would enjoy only when we were entertaining guests. Even then, Mum would cut a whole chicken into four portions, and bake one of those quarters to share among ten or twelve people.

Cooking was done on the top of a large lantern filled

with oil, which doubled as a heater. It was smelly and we used to get headaches from the heavy fumes. It was a relief when it was later replaced with a cooker-heater run off a gas cylinder. Over the years we were living at the garden we gradually evolved our traditional rural Afghan ways, to incorporate some of the more modern amenities available in urban Iran. We had electricity, and began to acquire a few appliances, such as a radio and cassette player. Eventually, we even bought a refrigerator, but this was a big expense, costing my father the equivalent of three months' wages.

My mother spent a lot of time with the owner's wife, who we called Nana Haji. Mum used to help her in the kitchen, and with looking after her children and grandchildren. This way, she learned to speak the local dialect, and found out a lot about Iranian culture and city life. Mum even went so far as to change her name, from the more traditional Afghan Narma to a popular Iranian name, Fatima, as a way of fitting in. Not only that, but Nana Haji taught her how to cook some Iranian dishes. She was kind to me too, asking me to do odd jobs such as sweeping the yard, and then making sure to pay me good pocket-money. My brother Mohammad Baqer and sister Masumeh and I became good friends with the owner's children and grandchildren, who treated us as equals. Through conversations with them, I learned to adjust to the Tehran dialect.

It was not only the language that was unfamiliar. We had never encountered Coca-Cola before, and I remember how strange the flavour was. Later, it became a favourite drink. And then there were the oranges.

We didn't have oranges back home, but there were oranges in the market, and my dad brought some home one day. He

43

offered these strange objects to my mum and aunt, to see what would happen. Of course, they tried to eat them whole, biting into the peel then thrusting the fruit aside in disgust. 'So bitter! How can you eat such a thing!' My father coolly picked one up, peeled it, and ate it segment by segment in front of them, looking very pleased with himself.

During our first summer in the garden, the neighbours told my mum that she should register me for school, as I would be seven years old in August. My hours at school would be determined by a timetable drawn up in accordance with Muslim prescription, with boys and girls taught separately. One week we girls would be taught on the morning shift, from 7:30 to 12:30, with boys attending in the afternoon; the following week the shifts would be swapped over, and I'd find myself at school between 1:00 and 6:00 in the afternoon.

We had no money for uniforms, but the school allowed me to wear what I had. So I arrived at my first class in a frumpy knee-length brown dress, with a pattern of flowers. Instead of a satchel, I had an old businessman's attaché case, all metal clasps and square corners, which had belonged to Baba Haji's son. And on my feet I wore some ugly boy's shoes that were the cast-offs of one of Baba Haji's grandsons. I felt conspicuous and embarrassed.

But I needn't have worried. The teachers were so kind and friendly, and the children got used to me so quickly, that I forgot any inhibitions. I did well, learned fast, made friends, and soon became a favourite in the class. But there was one occasion when I took my wish to impress almost too far. I had been drawing some pictures in my exercise book, when my mum picked it up, had a look at what I'd done, and drew a flower for me. When the teacher, Ms Bastani, saw it later, she asked me if I had drawn it myself. Seizing on this opportunity to make an impression, I said 'Yes.' So she asked me to go outside the classroom and make another drawing of a flower. She must have suspected that it was too good to be mine. I made another drawing on the back of my mum's, tracing the shape of the flower through the paper, and colouring it in as neatly as I could. Even I could see it was not as good as my mum's drawing. I didn't deserve to get away with this naive ruse, but the teacher responded in exactly the right way, with words of encouragement, instead of embarrassing me. She went on to become headteacher, and an important figure in my education.

Out of school I would help Mum, or look after my younger siblings, or give Dad a hand in the garden. In the evenings there was homework to do, and my dad used to help me with literacy and numeracy. I remember, in my first year, the teacher announcing that anyone who did very well would be awarded twenty, meaning a top mark. I made the faux pas of going to the front of the class to collect my award, thinking the 'twenty' she had referred to meant something like twenty chocolates. But I progressed well, and in the second year became top student.

We kept in touch with family members still in Afghanistan, but communication was cumbersome. There was no telephone, so we wrote letters, or recorded messages on cassette tapes and sent them home with visitors. We would receive taped greetings in reply, and I remember Mum and Dad crying when they listened to the voices of loved ones far away. We children were too young to understand why our parents were homesick, and my mum tried to explain that I would only know what it was like when I found myself in a similar situation. Many years later, her words would come true.

My dad found a picture of Iran's supreme leader, Ayatollah Khomeini, from a calendar I think, and put it on the wall. This was in part from respect, and acceptance of the Ayatollah as a religious leader. It was also, perhaps, a gesture of our wish to be integrated. (Later, in 1989 when the Ayatollah died, we all gathered at the house of our neighbour, who had one of the few televisions in the area, to watch the live broadcast of the funeral.) But what mattered more was the uncanny resemblance between the Ayatollah and my grandfather, Mum's dad. We had had to leave him behind, and if I think about what I missed most about Afghanistan in those early days in Tehran, it was him. So whenever I looked at that picture of the Ayatollah, I thought of my beloved granddad.

One of the saddest days of my young life came in my third year at school, when we received the news that my grandfather had died. A day of mourning would have been customary, but our new circumstances were different. I went to school, my dad went to work, and it was not until the evening that we went to my aunt's for the family to mourn together. And at the end of the evening my father insisted we return home, so that he was ready for work in the morning, and I was ready for school. I never missed a day at school, not even when I fell ill and found myself falling asleep in class.

Sometimes we would stand in the garden near the mulberry tree, and watch rockets and missiles flying over, heading towards the city centre – for Iran was of course at war with Iraq. The war had begun in 1980, with Saddam Hussein's invasion and capture of territory in Iran's south-western Khuzestan province. The invading forces were later driven out, and Iraq sued for peace, but Iran opted to prolong the war in the hope of driving Saddam from power. By the time we came to Tehran, the war had settled into a stalemate. Combat was pursued as it had been in the First World War, by trench warfare conducted across a static battle front along Iraq's border, giving rise to heavy casualties for negligible gain. At the same time, both sides engaged in sporadic air and missile attacks against military and economic targets, as well as terrorising strikes on cities and their civilian populations. The Iraqi attacks on Tehran were what we witnessed, from time to time, from the safe haven of the garden. I remember whenever there was a red alarm, people would come out of the city centre to take shelter in public buildings, such as the schools and mosques. Some of them would come into our garden, to wait until the all-clear was sounded.

Everyone was encouraged to contribute to the war effort. Like many people, Baba Haji used to send donations to the military, in support of the war against Iraq. He had a personal investment in this, as his second youngest son was in the army, fighting at the frontier. At my school, we were given piggy banks which we were supposed to take home, and bring back to school filled with coins. We had no spare money at home, and I could not fill my piggy bank, so worried I might be chastised for not sufficiently supporting the country which had adopted me. The school also gave pupils a bag to fill with food or other provisions, to send to the fighting troops. We had nothing to spare, but my father thought that they would need not only bodily sustenance but spiritual guidance too, so put one of his copies of the Qur'an in the bag.

When I moved up to Year 4 at the age of ten, I found the class was housed in a new building. Instead of benches, we all had to sit on the floor. That was not the only change. Our new teacher very shortly began to treat us as if we were her servants, giving us duties such as being sent to the bakery to buy her bread. If a pupil failed to complete their homework, she would punish them by slotting pens between their fingers, then squeezing their hands painfully tight. Or she would tug at a pupil's hair, even dragging them by the hair across the floor. A lot of the pupils began to dread going to school, lost any enthusiasm they might have had, and struggled to learn. One of those girls was a neighbour of ours, from an Afghan family, and her marks suffered, often being less than ten out of twenty. So when she took her results home to show her parents, she would write a '1' before her mark, a score of 7/20 becoming 17/20. At the end of term, of course, the teacher found out, and the girl was severely punished, being quite badly bruised as a result. Despite the cruelty of the teacher, I never lost my enthusiasm for school, and was still eager to learn.

One day, while I was still in this trying year at school, I came home as usual, did my homework, played with Masumeh outside, then helped Mum prepare dinner. After dinner, I was alone with my parents, when my dad leaned over to my mum and said: 'I think it's time.' She nodded, silently. Dad turned back to me. 'There is something we need to tell you.' And when I heard what he had to say, I felt my lovely world reeling and collapsing around me.

4

The mulberry tree

MY COUSIN MOHAMMAD Hassan, the younger son of my father's eldest brother, had been giving me unusually generous gifts for a while: some beautiful notebooks and a lovely set of colouring pens, even a real silver watch. I was grateful, thinking that this was kindness, and nothing more. But then my father asked me if I remembered the story of what had happened when I was born.

'Yes', I replied, 'I know the story.' My uncle had wished for me to fill the place of his deceased daughter, in some spiritual way. To mark this, he had insisted on choosing my name, Shakardokht.

'So he did', said my father. 'That is true. But there was something else your uncle did, something you haven't been told until today. When you were born, he put a mark against your name, to signify that you had been chosen.'

Chosen? That could mean only one thing. Chosen in marriage. My uncle's son, Mohammad Hassan, was twelve years older than me, and had been waiting to marry me all these years. But what did I have in common with him? Nothing. The idea that I was to marry him, that this had been somehow agreed behind my back, that I was expected to be compliant and deferential: all of this came as a complete shock to me. I didn't know what to think, and there seemed to be nobody I could talk to. Instead, I took these dark moments to the shade of my mulberry tree. During our time in the garden, this had become my special place; now, as I was growing up, I would go to the tree to share whatever I had on my mind, and in this way, it became almost my confidante.

Nothing more happened until I was fourteen years old, by then in secondary school. I came home from school one day to be met by my father, who told me we had visitors. He invited me to join them inside the house, which was very strange. I couldn't understand why he was being so formal, sycophantic almost, in the way he ushered me inside, especially when I found it was only my uncle, aunt and cousins.

My uncle came straight to the point. They needed to officially take me to their home, as now was the time I should get married. I discovered that they were already planning the ceremony together, and when I arrived, had been compiling lists of the names of wedding invitees.

I was distraught, and confused, and went out to the garden, to my constant mulberry tree. My father came out and found me sitting on one of the branches.

'You look so upset', he said, 'when this should be a time of celebration. What is on your mind? Are you unhappy?'

We talked about the coming marriage, and he was sympathetic to my misgivings, saying that knowing my personality – and the personalities of the uncle and aunt, and of the cousin – he could not really see how the marriage was going to work. What was more, he conceded that as a baby I had not been in a position to make any promises. This was good. He was on my side, and he would support my objections to the marriage. But then reality kicked in. Etiquette, he reminded me, forbade him from contradicting his older brother, because he was patriarch of the family. So he went back inside to rejoin the family committee, who were taking it upon themselves to make so many important decisions, on my behalf and – although they might not have known it – against my will.

I decided that my best course of action was to explain to my cousin why I was not happy with the idea of the marriage. So I went into the kitchen, and wrote a letter telling him what was on my mind. The age gap between us, I began, was too great. The lives he and I intended for ourselves were incompatible. What I wanted was to study, and to have a career; what he was looking for was a housewife, who would give him children, and care for him and for his parents. I suggested there were loads of girls who would be very happy to marry someone in his position, but I was not one of them. He would do better to find somebody else to marry, and leave me alone. Although he had the authority to force me into marriage, I begged him not to, and warned him that if he did, there would be dire consequences: it would turn his life, and mine – I chose my words deliberately – into a living hell. I signed off by wishing him a happy life, and hoping that he would find another girl.

Early the next day, when I gave the letter to my cousin, he must have assumed it was a love letter. He blushed and put it into his pocket, and soon after he and his family returned home, taking the letter with them, still unread.

On the following morning, I was busy in the garden when my older cousin Mohammad Hussein arrived, in a very angry mood. I opened the gate to him and he brushed past me, without saying a word, and stormed over to where my dad was at work. He confronted my father, shaking the letter in his face, saying 'What is this?', and shouting: 'You do not even have control of your daughter. Shame on you! See what she has written to my brother!' My father calmly replied: 'We call ourselves Muslims, and in Islam, forced marriage is not permitted. If my daughter is not happy, what can I do about it?' The cousin had no answer to that, and stomped out of the garden, still furious.

It was two weeks before we heard from my uncle. Was my rejected cousin pining for me? Not quite. In that short time, another girl had been found for him; a wedding had been arranged; and already the marriage ceremony was imminent. Despite the hostility from my uncle and aunt, and although we were not invited, my father insisted that we attend the wedding. He reasoned that it was not good to prolong ill feeling, and our family must stay together, having nobody else in the country. My dad held true to this conviction, so that henceforth we always did the right thing by visiting my uncle and aunt on any appropriate occasion. His overtures were not reciprocated by my uncle and aunt, who not only made us unwelcome, but tried to persuade other members of the wider family to have nothing to do with me or my parents.

A few months after the wedding, my uncle was working in the fields when there was an Iraqi bombing raid, and he was struck by shrapnel and wounded. My father took the opportunity of visiting him in hospital, when he tried to effect a reconciliation, with partial success. Relations between my parents with my uncle and aunt improved after this, but on family visits the cousins were still very rude, especially towards me.

I consoled myself with the thought that this situation was much better than what might have been. I still had, after all, my precious independence. But then, one year after the departure of Mohammad Hassan, my father picked another cousin for me to marry.

Mohammed Amin was then around twenty years old. He was an only child, whose father was my mum's brother, and whose mother was my dad's sister. Since the mother had passed away, my father felt responsible for the son. He suggested to me that because the boy had nobody else in his life, he would make a good and devoted husband. We'll see, I thought.

Mohammed Amin visited us as a guest, and I had a chance to get to know him. One evening, he came into the room when I was watching one of my favourite TV programmes. We had not long acquired our first TV set, a small 14-inch screen black-and-white model, and I loved two Japanese series in particular. *Haniko* and *Oshin* both tell rags-to-riches stories of strong-willed girls who want to prioritise careers over marriage, – a sentiment that I strongly identified with. I can't remember what I was watching on this occasion, but Mohammed Amin glanced at the screen, and abruptly changed the channel to something he preferred to watch, without asking me. It was one of those lightbulb moments: I knew for certain, there and then, that there was no chance of a happy future for the two of us together. If he was prepared to ignore my wishes in this way, to overrule me, so early on when we were still getting to know each other – at a time when he might be expected to be showing an interest in me and my tastes – how could I ever hope to be heard by him in years to come?

But with my father still encouraging him, the cousin proposed, and brought the money for an engagement party. My father threatened that if I didn't accept the proposal, he would disown me. This left me in a conundrum: how could I say 'no' to the proposal, without saying 'goodbye' to my father? I didn't know how to respond. I was so anxious for guidance that I even wrote to an agony uncle on a radio station, but he did not respond to my letter in time. So I drew up my own strategy: I told my father that I would accept my cousin's offer of marriage, on condition that I would be allowed to attend high school for three years. The normal duration of high school at the time was four years, but by self-study, and sitting the end-of-second-year exam at the end of year one, I would aim to skip a year. Meanwhile I would be engaged, but not married. The advantages of this arrangement were that it would allow me a decent length of time to consider the marriage proposal; my father would not disown me; and I would have the completion of my higher education guaranteed by our engagement contract.

My father told the cousin, who accepted, and brought the required money to my father on the Thursday night. The engagement would be celebrated the following Tuesday, to coincide with the religious ceremony marking mid-Sha'ban: this marks the birthday of the twelfth disciple, the prophet Muhammad al-Mahdi.

On the Friday, Mohammed Amin was feeling very happy and went to share the good news with his uncle, Mohammad Ali, father of the cousin I had originally been going to marry. He was particularly close to this 'double uncle' who was both his mum's brother and the husband of his dad's sister. But instead of congratulations, the uncle rounded on him: 'Didn't you learn the lesson from us? We waited fourteen years. She tells you she will marry you, then she will reject you after three years.'

The cousin returned the following day in a more sombre mood, and told my father he would only let me continue my education if I signed the marriage contract. I wouldn't have to move into his house; he would let me continue to live in the home of my father, and complete my education. It worried me that if this happened there would be no escape route for me: I would be tied in contract to marry the cousin, even after my prospects had been improved by my education. So I asked my father how long it had been since they shook hands on their now-broken agreement, and he concurred it was two days. I pointed out sharply: 'In that case, what guarantees would there be that he would allow me three years to complete my studies?'

I got my way. Mohammed Amin took back his money, and the marriage agreement was broken off. With it went my guarantee of higher education. My father, no doubt pricked by this latest turn of events, told me to forget about school. What I needed was to get married. Even though he had been himself a teacher of girls, he told me that this was an end to my secondary education; I had already reached a sufficient level of learning. So he stopped me from going to high school.

At that time my younger sister Hakima was seven years old and due to begin her schooling. It happened that her Year 1, and the high school I was to attend, were being taught in the same building, on different morning and afternoon shifts. So when I took Hakima to register at school, I met my old teacher, Ms Bastani, who had been so encouraging in my first year at school. She was now headteacher. She wanted to know why I was not sitting in my class. I started to cry and could not explain, but she confided that my friends had already told her the reason: I was not at school because my father would not allow me to come.

When I told her I needed to register Hakima, she looked me in the eye and told me that: 'Unfortunately, this will not be possible. A parent – your father – has to come to school to complete registration.' I suspected that this was her stratagem for confronting him.

When I told my dad, he was suspicious. 'Why do they want me to come to school? Is it that you have reported me, for keeping you away from school?' I breezily said: 'No, nothing like that. It's just a regulation that you need to go to register Hakima yourself.' At registration, the headteacher cornered him, asking why he sent the little one to school when he wouldn't let her best pupil attend, because I was the top student in the class. My father began to make excuses, one after another. Finance. Culture. Marriage. Each time, Ms Bastani had an answer to his objections. In the end, she persuaded him to let me attend for just one more year.

When my father returned home, he said: 'OK, let's get ready to go and buy you the books for your year at school.' In Iranian education, high-school students have to provide their own books. At the educational bookshop, I moved deftly among the bookshelves, picking out all the books I would need for the next two years. My brother, Mohammad Baqer, was also there, buying his own school books and stationery, and he turned to me and asked, in an unnecessarily loud voice: 'Why are you buying books for two years? You're only allowed to attend school for one more year.' I thought that if he was trying to catch me out, in front of our dad, I could play that game too. So I said loudly enough for our father to hear: 'They might be able to stop me from going to school for the second year, but they can't stop me from attending second-year exams. So I need books for both years.'

At school, I studied for years one and two in the same year. At the end of the first year, a pass mark of 80% qualified students to sit the second-year exam. At this stage we were streamed into two groups; students with higher scores tended to be placed in the natural sciences stream, while the remainder went into humanitarian studies. I was selected for natural sciences. I didn't get much encouragement at home for my studies, and was lucky to have such a dedicated headteacher in Ms Bastani.

During the summer at the end of my first year in high school, we had a visitor to our house. It was the last person I would have expected to see again: Mohammed Amin. He apologised, and told me he accepted all my conditions. I said: 'No, I'm sorry, but I don't accept your proposal any more.' What had changed my mind? It was, perhaps, the discovery that the conditions I had asked to be written into our contract regarding education no longer applied. Since my schooling was continuing, and my father had not disowned me, I did not need any contract to protect my immediate concerns. With that out of the way, I reminded myself that, right from the start, I had ruled out marriage to a husband who would swap TV channels without asking.

When I told my father, he became extremely angry, and repeated his diktat: either I married the cousin, or he would disown me and I would have to leave his house. I stood my ground, and said: 'Look, Father, God gave you children to raise, but not the authority to direct the rest of their lives.' At this he became even angrier, and grabbed the yard broom and tried to sweep me away, saying: 'Get out of my house. You're not my daughter any more!'

By this time, we had moved from the nursery garden that had been our home. We were now living next door to a new factory under construction, where my father was working as a security guard. The surrounding ground was being resurfaced; some of it exposed sharp hardcore, the rest freshly-laid tarmac. When I ran out of the house, I was barefoot, running over red-hot stones and bitumen from the road surfacing, with my father chasing me with the broom. We ran round and round in circles, round the water tank, my feet burning all the way. Eventually, I tired him out because I was faster than him, and he couldn't catch me. He went back indoors, shouting out to me not to return.

I didn't know what to do, or where to go. Had I been disowned by my father? Was I forbidden from ever again setting foot in the family home? I sat down next to the water tank, to collect my thoughts. My mum came out with some food for me, but said very little. She simply put the food down beside me and went back into the house. That night I slept outside in the yard.

The next day, when my dad went to work, I ventured back indoors. I stayed out in the yard again that night, but was too scared to sleep. By the second day it felt as though perhaps the storm was abating, so I remained in the house. But my father would no longer speak to me directly, would no longer even use my name, instead commanding my mother to 'tell your daughter' this, 'tell your daughter' that!

The night before I was due to return to school for the new term, I had a dream. At first, all was darkness. Then, on a distant horizon, appeared a bright spot of light, which gradually grew in intensity and came nearer. It revealed itself as a verse from the Qur'an, which translates as: 'By the pen which writes.' This is the recognition in the Qur'an that it is the act of writing that allows the scripture to come down to us unchanged. For this reason, Allah swears by the pen, and what is written with the pen. Of course, I knew that although I was writing with a pen, as a part of my education, you could not exactly say that I was therefore 'doing God's work'. But it did make me feel that what I was doing was in some way prescribed. My own interpretation of the dream was that it meant that nothing – and nobody – would stand in the way of my education. It made me all the more determined.

So the next morning, I put on my school dress to attend the start of Year 2, and appeared for breakfast, where my father was sitting. I felt like a mouse in front of a cat. But he paid me no attention, and I took this to mean that he was going to raise no objections.

At school, I was fortunate to be allocated to a very popular literacy teacher, Mrs Maliha Shakoori. During breaks, instead of socialising with the other teachers, she would come into the school yard and chat with the students. When I explained my problems, her understanding and support gave me the confidence to pursue my studies to the end. At the start of the next school holidays she gave me a notebook, and when I opened it I found she had pasted a poem inside the front cover. It related the story of how Joseph was separated from his father Jacob, who loved him dearly, and sold by his jealous brothers into slavery in Egypt. He rose to become appointed governor of Egypt by the Pharaoh, when he was visited by his repentant brothers and joyously reunited with his father.

In my country, we have a culture of opening a book and taking divination from whatever is read first. Mrs Shakoori knew this, and must have known that the first thing I would read in my new notebook would be the poem, and that I would understand its symbolism and take heart from its message of reconciliation.

My mother remarked to me that relatives and neighbours were talking about me behind my back, saying that I was getting older and girls of my age should be getting married. She said it was making difficulties for her and my father, and they could not go on like this. My younger cousin's wife, too, began to encourage me to marry. By this time, I was feeling under so much pressure that I was having thoughts of suicide.

And then, with singularly bad timing, came another proposal of marriage.

5

To see inside the body

MY ELDER COUSIN, MOHAMMAD Hussein, was already married.
He and his wife had been married for twelve years, loved each
other, and led what appeared to be a harmonious existence;
but for one impediment. They had had no children. So now,
he was proposing to take me as his second wife. He would set
me up in a separate house, so I would not have to cross paths
with his first wife. In return, I could give him babies.

By this arrangement, it would be possible for him to
avoid the stigma of divorce. In our society, marriage is
seen as a lifelong bond, even if the relationship is abusive.
Divorce represents failure, and worse: it is considered an
act of immorality, bringing dishonour on both parties.
After a divorce, a girl's own family may not accept her
back, according to the adage: 'We send a daughter out in a

wedding gown, and take her back in a coffin.' I had known Mohammad Hussein a long time, and irrespective of my feelings about becoming his second wife, I believed him to be a good and honourable man. I could understand how important it would be for him to avoid divorce, to protect his wife's interests as much as his own.

The kind of polygyny my cousin was proposing was legal and permissible under Sharia law. Men may take up to four wives, whom the law stipulates should be treated as equals. Wealthy men are more likely to take advantage of this arrangement, as a means of acquiring land, property and wealth, not to mention heirs. It also occurs commonly when a married man is under obligation to take the widow of a dead brother as his second wife, a situation presented to – and rejected by – my great-grandmother. The third instance is when there is infertility within a marriage. It is entirely characteristic of our patriarchal culture that whenever this occurs, there is a presumption that it must be the woman, not the man, who is sterile.

The proposal was put to me in the formal manner, with a visit from the cousin in company with his father and mother, as well as his younger brother and sister-in-law. The brother, of course, was Mohammad Hassan, to whom I had been promised at birth. Regardless of our turbulent past, I was good friends with his wife, now the mother of two children. I managed to find a private moment to speak to her in confidence, thinking she might drop her guard and tell me this marriage was not such a good idea. Quite the opposite: she tried to persuade me into seeing this as an advantageous proposal because, she argued, it would offer a better environment and quality of life than I enjoyed living in my father's house. Such was the state I was in, so wracked with uncertainties, so punch-drunk from the people I loved and cared about trying to dissuade me from my own intuitions, that I gave the proposal serious consideration.

The family group went to speak first to my father, who told them melodramatically: 'She is no longer my daughter!', so they would have to speak to me directly. I was outside, and Mohammad Hussein came out and sat beside me. He was somebody I had always respected, for his wisdom and his logic, and he had always encouraged me. I suppose I regarded him as something like a senior brother. But now, when he was so close beside me, I was shocked to see what an age he looked. Did I really have to marry someone so much older – sixteen *years* – than me? And how could I envisage that my needs, as a second wife, would ever come first? I wondered what would happen if I were to marry him, in the hope of having children with him, and that didn't happen. What if we discovered that the failure of his first marriage was due to his own inability to become a father, so that I was condemned to never becoming a mother?

He outlined his proposal, and I told him I would think about it. That was good enough, for now at least; the cousin must have thought his overture had been at least partially successful, as before long, once again, I started to receive some rather nice presents.

But then my younger sister Hakima fell ill. She was nine years old, and had a cockerel that she kept as a pet. She loved it as much as any more conventional pet, such as a cat or a dog. Unfortunately, the cockerel had the annoying habit of pecking anybody it didn't know, including some of the people working at the factory, who complained about it to my dad. This situation somehow exasperated my father so much that one day he slaughtered the creature. I suppose he had grown up knowing this to be the expected fate of any cockerel, and failed to make allowance for the special status of this particular bird.

My mum was the first to notice that there was something wrong with Hakima. At breakfast, she was having trouble holding a spoon, and spilled food on herself. Mum asked her one morning if she had washed her face. Hakima said 'yes', but it was a lie. She couldn't wash her face because she was unable to control her hand. She did her best to cover it up, but she was becoming paralysed down her right side. Before long the paralysis caused her to develop a severe limp, and she had to stop going to school.

We took her to the hospital, but they were unable to make a diagnosis. They recommended a magnetic resonance imaging (MRI) scan, in which the patient lies inside a tube where strong magnetic fields and radio waves produce detailed images of the inside of the body. It was hoped this would uncover some internal medical condition of Hakima's that could not be deduced from a normal examination.

There were at that time only two MRI scanners in the country, and the cost of having a scan commensurately high, at 90,000 Iranian tomans. (The toman is the everyday unit of currency in Iran, equal to ten rials.) This was at a time when my father's wage was 15,000 tomans per month. It put him into a predicament, which came out when his employer, Amir Nowruzi, questioned him about Hakima's crisis. When Dad explained what the hospital had recommended, and what a difficult position he found himself in, to his amazement Amir generously offered to cover the cost of diagnosis.

My mum was at this time pregnant, so it fell to me to take Hakima to the hospital for her scan. They kept her in for one week, under observation. The MRI scans, blood test and all other results were normal. Nevertheless, the doctors gave her medication, and when we got her home, she gradually began to recover. It took about three months for her to regain full movement of her limbs. But before her illness, she had been the top student at school. Now, she lost concentration and her marks dropped.

We still can't know what exactly had happened to Hakima. Was this simply a physiological episode that had somehow evaded diagnosis? Or had the fate of her cockerel triggered something more than mere upset, an effect closer to a profound trauma? Was the help she had needed not so much medical as psychiatric?

While I was in the hospital caring for Hakima, I found myself getting very involved in all the assessments, and wanting to learn more about the ingenious ways in which medical conditions could be diagnosed and treated. In particular, I was fascinated by the MRI technology and its capabilities. How was it possible to make such detailed images of the patient, without causing harm? In my curiosity I must have fired off questions at the consultant, who took them entirely in his stride. What he told us seemed to me extraordinary. In every part of our bodies, he explained, there is a high proportion of water, made up of hydrogen and oxygen atoms. Within each hydrogen atom is a particle called a proton, which is very sensitive to magnetic fields. What happens when you lie inside the scanner is that electro-magnets are switched on, creating a magnetic field which aligns those protons. Then, radio waves are fired at whichever part of the body is being examined. These waves interfere with the magnetism, flipping the protons out of alignment. It was what happens next that took my breath away. The radio waves are turned off, the protons realign, and in so doing, radio signals are transmitted from the protons. And these signals, of different types and durations, contain a wealth of information about the locations of different types of tissue in the body. They are picked up by receivers and converted into detailed images of the inside of the body.

I found myself thinking fast: the idea of creating pictures of the inside of the body like this was something I would love to know more about. Why didn't I study it, perhaps even at university? I could see this shaping my vocation, my future…

I was in the midst of this reverie when the phone rang. Our landline telephone was a recent innovation, which had been installed for my dad's job in the factory. It was the first time we had ever had a phone, and friends and I used to call each other in the evenings to chat about exams and homework. This particular call was not one of those friends, but my cousin Mohammad Hussein phoning to ask how Hakima was doing. He reminded me that he had paid me to make him some ribbon flowers, one of the spare-time activities – dress-making was another – that I used to undertake to raise a little money for my education. He had wanted the flowers in time for Nowruz, the new year festivities of 21 March, and I had to apologise that I'd been unable to make them in time because of the hospital trip. He replied: 'Don't worry at all, you can bring the flowers when you come to live in my home permanently.' I took a deep breath, and said: 'I'm sorry, but I've thought about this, and I cannot accept your proposal.' My cousin must have heard the finality in the tone of my voice, because the subject of our marriage was never raised again.

It was not that I was opposed to marriage on principle; in fact I had, for some time, been actively thinking about how I might meet a suitable man. Some relatives had a son who was a high-school student, so at a family marriage ceremony I connived to sit next to his mum. It was not difficult to steer the conversation round to her son's education, and his prospects, and the fact that they were looking for a girl for him. I liked what she told me about him, and felt comfortable with the fact that he was just one year older than me. I must have expressed my enthusiasm, as it was a matter of weeks before their family paid a visit to ours. It was done in a casual way, dropping-by without any formal arrangement, but the fact that the entire family arrived at our door suggested it was not without purpose.

When I met the son I found him likeable enough. But on reflection, I was concerned that a wedding would be too early for both of us; that he was too young to have proven himself. Who knew how much closer, or more distant, our respective futures would lie after we had each completed our education?

The family sent their son-in-law to present a formal proposal of marriage. He was somebody we knew well, as he had been one of my father's students back in our home village. When he arrived, my father came out with his slightly aggrieved speech about me not being his daughter any more, and how the son-in-law would need to speak to me directly. I listened to what the man had to say, and answered by telling him that I would like time to consider the proposal. He stayed for dinner, then left with my non-committal response.

There were so many considerations to be weighed up. Not just the question of whether it was too soon, but my own responsibilities: for one, my mum was pregnant again and would need my help; another, I was trying to help Hakima get back on course with her schoolwork. My decision made, I thought I should share it at once, as a way of ridding myself of its burden. In the normal course of events I would have spoken to my father, but he was still not talking to me directly. So I wrote him a letter, which I left for him to discover on the windowsill that he used as a kind of makeshift office. I explained that because of my commitments at home and at school, my answer to the proposal was 'no'. But unknown to me, my dad did not notice the letter, and remained unaware of my decision.

The son-in-law returned a fortnight later. I helped prepare a meal for our guest, and while that was cooking I served tea. When I brought it in, he asked me directly: 'Well, we have given you two weeks, have you thought about this matter?' I replied: 'Yes, I've thought about it carefully, and in my opinion it is too rushed to have the marriage now. If I finish school, and go to university, I may have better opportunities.' He became so angry that he didn't stay for dinner, didn't finish his tea, but abruptly got up and stormed out, not to return.

I had also been getting attention from some of the younger men who were work colleagues of my father in the factory, whom I discovered were secret admirers. One of them would come out of the factory when he saw me going to school and try to talk to me. He wrote a letter to me, which he gave to my brother to pass on, telling me that if I didn't accept his love, he was going to commit suicide.

Of course, I didn't accept his love or believe his threat, but it did strike me that this was not a good situation for me or for my next-oldest sister, Masumeh, who was by now also nearing eligible age. I raised my concerns with my mum, and suggested that to avoid further unwanted attention, we should find somewhere to live away from the factory. 'For instance', I said, 'we could go to the village where Auntie and Uncle are living and working.' I spelled out the benefits this would offer us all, of working in the fields and earning some money. What I didn't say was that I was secretly trying to save towards the fees for my entrance exam for university, and the income would be a godsend. Mum discussed my suggestion with my dad, who agreed, so early that summer the whole family, my dad excepted, took the journey of an hour or so to our new lodgings, a single rented room with open kitchen in Habib Abad village, a suburb of the city of Varamin, which lies about fifty miles south-east of Tehran. The children were registered in the local school, while Mum, my eldest brother, Mohammad Baqer, my eldest sister Masumeh and I soon found ourselves alongside our auntie's family, hard at work in the fields, on tasks like picking tomatoes and planting cucumbers.

We still felt the absences of my sister, Roqaya, who had died on the trek from Afghanistan, and a baby girl, Sakina, who had been stillborn after my mum was given the wrong medication. But by this time I had three brothers – Mohammad Baqer had been joined by the two youngest in the family, Ali Reza and Morteza – as well as my two sisters, Masumeh and Hakima, and it was perhaps seeing us all together, bursting out of our little rented room, that made my mum decide that the family was big enough. She made an appointment with the hospital, requesting surgery to block her fallopian tubes, so that she would no longer be able to give birth.

This may seem an unlikely proposition, given the patriarchal nature of Iran's governance. But things had changed since the death of Ayatollah Khomeini in 1989. The new Supreme Leader, Ayatollah Ali Khamenei, had served previously as president, where he had proved rather ineffectual. But the incoming president, cleric Ali Akbar Hashemi Rafsanjani, was a moderniser who instigated a programme of economic and social reform. On the face of it this appeared a liberal move, although in reality it was motivated by a pragmatic conservatism. The networks of roads, electricity, water and telephones were to be extended to the poorer rural areas. And there was a programme of education on sexual health and family planning, with free condoms and affordable contraceptives, and supportive laws. Under the slogan 'two children is enough', voluntary sterilisation was available on demand, as were subsidised vasectomies. Much of this would be withdrawn in subsequent years, from government concern at the prospect of an ageing population.

Although the treatment Mum wanted was available, the hospital told her that they could only carry out the procedure with the consent of my dad. But to my surprise, Mum took charge of the situation. Dad would probably not give permission, she explained, and she could not face another pregnancy: she had had enough children, and needed her strength to take care of those she already had. The hospital was persuaded, and the operation went ahead. I admired her for standing her ground. It was heartening to find that, in a society where prejudices against women are often dressed up as laws and rules, or conventions and habits, sometimes a strong woman's voice, her wishes and her rights, could still be heard.

Dad had initially stayed behind to work in the factory, and we used to go back to visit him at weekends. After a few months he got fed up with this arrangement, gave up his job, and joined us. He went back to the routine of visiting the square, this time not in central Tehran but Varamin, in search of labouring jobs in construction or farming, most of them poorly paid. Eventually, he found a steady job at a garage. He began in the workshops repairing cars, but when the owner learned of Dad's skills he offered him a job on his farm, where Dad would work during the week, returning home for weekends.

That summer of 1995, I felt back in control of my life. There were no marriage proposals hanging over me. I was earning money. My high-school education was coming to an end, and I had mentally cleared some space to study for, and take, the competitive concours entrance exam to university. I was eighteen years old.

6

A home-made lantern

THE CONCOURS UNIVERSITY ENTRANCE exam would be my toughest challenge yet. Tough not least because of the conditions at home, where my father was still not talking to me. It felt as though everything I did was testing the limits of his patience, and there might be an explosion at any time. 'Tell your daughter this. University is a red line; the limit', he would say to my mother. But to my way of thinking, the red line would be *not* going to university.

I realised that the only way to prepare myself for the exam without provoking my father's wrath would be to study in secret. So I made a lantern, with an old syrup bottle filled with oil as fuel, and some cotton yarn as a wick. Then, at night, when all the lights were off, I would get out of bed and sit in a corner of the garden with my lantern, trying to memorise every line of reasoning in every one of my books. On cold nights, I would use the bathroom as my study, hoping that nobody would need to use it. Luckily, I never got caught.

The examination was a challenge academically, too. It was at a standard well beyond the normal scope of high-school teaching, and it was left to examinees to make what arrangements they could to prepare themselves. My brother Mohammad Baqer very kindly came to my aid, lending me his savings so that I could pay for the exam registration and buy a set of ten years' sample exam papers. Then I set to, testing myself on responding to the multiple-choice questions under my own simulated 'exam conditions'. But would that be enough? The concours was so very competitive. Towards the end of the school year, my classmates had been talking themselves up, boasting about signing up to cramming courses 'with the most successful track records in the city!', or saying they had a tutor who was 'the best!' I felt very disadvantaged, lost my confidence, and began to believe that I could not pass the exam. All my peers were getting such specialised preparation, and there was me, studying by myself, by the light of a home-made lantern.

I managed to get through the first stage, with a good score. This was the point at which my father started work on the garage owner's farm and was away from home during the week, so immediately conditions at home were more relaxed. It was such a relief to be able to continue to study for the final stage without looking over my shoulder all the time, without my crazy clandestine night-time routine.

In the event, I was the only girl in the school that year who managed to pass the exam and get a university place. I became known as 'the university girl', as news of my success spread by word of mouth. In a way, I became locally famous. This was a great boost to my confidence; and such a contrast to the reaction to a separate recent triumph at school. What had happened was that another Afghan girl and I had been selected to represent the province at a national schools' competition. A teacher who was supposed to accompany us to the venue failed to appear, so I went to the headteacher, Mrs Tehrani, to ask what was happening. She told me she couldn't spare a teacher to take 'two Afghan students', as if to underline our inferior status. I asked her if the two of us could travel alone, to which she agreed. We took a taxi to the contest, and we both won prizes! Normally, such prizes would be presented ceremonially at school, but in our case that did not happen. Instead, when we went to collect our final-year exam results, we were pointed towards a corner of the room. 'Oh, by the way, those are your awards from the contest. Go and get them.'

When it came to choosing university subjects, I had opted for medicine. I fostered the idea that I would love to return to the Afghan villages when qualified, to vaccinate children against measles. Equally, I was still fired with the curiosity about radiology that had come about when Hakima had her MRI scan. In the admissions process, it was the latter that won the upper hand, and I was accepted by Tehran University of Medical Sciences, to study radiation technology.

The reality of all this only struck me when I travelled with friends, two hours by bus, to the university campus. Arriving at the main gates, I felt awestruck. Everything looked so grand and important! The 1930s' architecture, a subtle mix of traditional Iranian and the European modernism of the time, with its reference to classical elements such as pillars and porticos, sent out a strong message of authority and permanence. It struck me that the purpose of this magnificence was to do more than simply impress: it was to showcase the power through knowledge imparted to those lucky enough to study there. People like me.

On my induction day, I learned that I was now part of the largest and most highly ranked medical university in Iran, boasting an impressive international reputation. The facilities extended to eleven schools, with no fewer than sixteen training hospitals, having a 4,000-bed capacity. There was an extensive Central Library and numerous faculty libraries within the schools and hospitals. And then there were the 70-odd research centres; the academic publishing programme, responsible for 58 journals… It was a hall of mirrors, endlessly multiplying.

But the lodgings brought me down to earth: dormitories with bunk beds, six students to a room, offering no more space or privacy than I'd had at home. I worked out that I could just survive by living on the tightest of budgets, eking out a meagre existence on some of the money I had saved from working in the summer vacation, picking cucumbers and tomatoes with my mum. She had also given me a little money of her own.

It took a few weeks before I felt ready to make my first visit back home. I had not received my father's blessing when I left for university, and was very wary of making contact again, not knowing what reception I might receive, and dreading the thought of his hostility. But I plucked up courage one weekend and caught the bus, picking my way rather slowly on the final stage of the route home from the bus stop.

As I neared the house, my father threw open the door.

'My daughter!'

'Dad!'

He opened his arms to welcome me, and I ran into his embrace.

What had happened to change his mind? I learned that an influential family friend from another city, Mr Salehi, had been in touch. My parents did not have a telephone, but he had called their landlord's number, and my dad had had to go running to take the call. Mr Salehi was engaged in education promotion, and was ringing to congratulate my father on my academic success. He tackled my dad's objections head-on, explaining that it would be useful and helpful for him to understand how important it was for me to go to university. On top of that, all the neighbours had been congratulating Dad on my success, and this had made him reconsider his attitude.

He later explained what had been troubling him, and why our relationship had gone so awry. To his mind, a refugee girl, coming from Afghanistan to Iran, could not possibly fight her way through the system to get to university without losing her ethical principles and values. And that, for my dad, meant to lose everything. If that had happened to me, if my ambition had obliterated everything of moral value that he had taught me, there would have been no option but for him to disown me. It was only once I had left home, giving him time to think and to listen to the accolades from Mr Salehi and the neighbours and friends, that he began to realise that perhaps he had got it wrong: I had reached university with my principles intact. That made him very proud. And so we became friends again.

We came closer together still when he needed an operation, and I took him to the hospital. Because I was studying radiation technology and it was a teaching hospital, the treatment was all for free. I was able to show off a little of my new-found skills by changing his dressing. He was grateful, and I could see he was thinking through everything that had happened. This led to a resolution that I thought wonderful at the time, and which impresses me still. He gathered the relatives together, and made a public apology in front of them all for how he had behaved towards me. It was a big, brave gesture. So affected was he by this change of heart that he went on to become an ambassador for girls' education. This would open the door for some of my other female relatives to go to university.

As Dad had reached out to me, so I reached out to him, listening again to his concerns that I should get married. I knew that from the way I had been rejecting so many unwanted marriage proposals, it might look as though I wished to avoid marriage altogether. In fact, nothing could be further from the truth. I was keen to be married, to enjoy a loving relationship and, God willing, to have children. But I was very aware that marriage is a life-changing commitment, not to be undertaken lightly.

So, I told Dad, I needed to be particular in my choice of husband. I believed I could only live harmoniously with somebody of my own background: one of the Afghan diaspora, a Shia, a Hazara. I felt that I could not – and did not want to – marry into an Iranian family, in part because of the endemic racism. Afghans were all too often regarded in this country as second-class citizens, as I frequently experienced at the bakery, where they tried to push me out of my place in the queue, with comments behind my back such as 'Afghan girl, what are you doing here? Go back to your own country if you want to buy bread.'

Not only that, but I was convinced that the right husband would be educated to the same level as me, if we were to live as equals. This was a task made more difficult because I was among the last intake of Afghans in Iran who managed to go to a school and get educated. From 1985, two years after we had entered the country, the only ID cards issued to refugees from Afghanistan by Iranians were temporary ones, which did not permit children to attend school.

By this time, 1996, the Soviet-Afghan war had come to an end, and the Iranian government was beginning to encourage refugees to return to their homelands. So the population of educated Afghans in the country was steadily shrinking. As for those who were eligible, the pool was smaller still. Of the ones of around my age, most of those who were educated were already married or engaged. There were many educated girls of my age who had had to compromise and marry uneducated boys.

During my first year at university, I would come home and find my mum crying. 'Why not? Why can't you marry?' If we had still been in Afghanistan, there would have been little I could have done about it, as proposals always come from the boy. But here in Iran it was different. If I found a suitable candidate, it would be perfectly acceptable for my father to voice the proposal. I took a pencil and scrap of paper, and drew up a shortlist of potential husbands, some of them brothers of my friends at school, one a distant relative. Then I began networking, trying to get to know their families.

Meanwhile, I was getting settled in at university. Despite

my misgivings at sharing a room with five others, we all got along well, because of similarities of family, culture and finance. Finance, or lack of it! Some days I had only enough money for the bus ticket to lectures, and my lunch. The rest of the day I fasted, with no breakfast or dinner. Fortunately, I ran into an old high school friend, Fatima Barbary, who was a year ahead of me at the university, and she advised me to apply for funding from the UNHCR. They run a scholarship programme known as DAFI (a German acronym which somehow unfolds in English as the Albert Einstein German Academic Refugee Initiative Fund). This offers refugee students such as me the possibility to fund an undergraduate degree in their country of asylum. I was even able to surprise my mum with money to pay her back for what she had lent me, which made her very happy.

By the time of my second year at university, I had re-established relations with my uncle's family, which was important because, since we were refugees, we didn't have many other relatives. I still wasn't warmly welcomed by my uncle and cousins, but was good friends with the girl who had married the first cousin instead of me. At her house, she said to me: 'Guess what? We had a guest from Mashhad today who is promoting education, Mr Salehi, and – wait till you hear this! – he had a boy with him who was studying at the university, and who was a religious school student too.'

Small world! This was the Mr Salehi, of course, who had brought my dad round to my way of thinking, and so was eternally 'a good man' in my books. And I have to say I very much liked the sound of 'the boy with him'. Here, at last, was someone who could conceivably tick all the boxes for a potential husband. I put him at the top of my shortlist, and thought about how I might get to meet him. And if that came to nothing, I was still trying to build up relations with the sisters and families of other boys I had on my list.

I reminded my mother that she had always wanted to return to the religious city of Mashhad, to go to Imam Reza's shrine, and I offered to take her there. There was enough money from the UNHCR scholarship to pay for the trip, not only for myself but for the tickets for my mother and my little brother. That left only the matter of accommodation. 'Perhaps we could stay,' I suggested, 'at Mr Salehi's house? That way, there would be no hotel expenses.'

This was not simply a case of me being presumptuous: on such a trip, especially one with a religious purpose, it was customary for Afghans visiting another city to stay at the house of a friend or relative, rather than in a hotel. Which was very convenient for me.

At the house of Mr Salehi, the conversation turned – naturally enough – to the subject of why I had not got married. Mr Salehi had been told of my track record of unsuccessful proposals, so I tried to put across my side of the story: it was not that I was picky, but the sort of a man I would like to marry would need to have a similar background, education and ethical values to myself. The man should be 'one of our own people', an Afghan, I explained again, because the racism I had experienced in Iran meant that I could not think of marrying an Iranian. The other attribute that mattered was that he should be kind. Well, said Mr Salehi's wife, Halima, I think we know of just such a boy! I did my best to show surprise, and tried to gauge the right expression of interest. I needed to appear positive enough, without being over-eager.

Halima told me a little of the boy's background. His family, like mine, were Afghan refugees to Iran. At the end of the Soviet war, they had judged it safe to return to their home city of Herat, leaving the boy to continue his studies in Iran. But the political situation in Afghanistan, instead of stabilising, had turned to civil war, as the mujahideen groups had fractured, and attempts to form a coalition government foundered. In this messy situation, a new militia – the Taliban – emerged, formed largely of Pashtun students (ṭālibs) from some of the madrasas, or religious schools.

They swept through the country, capturing first Kandahar, and in 1995, Herat. Now, in the summer of 1996, they were at the gates of Jalalabad, and it appeared inevitable that sooner or later Kabul itself would fall too.

Return to Afghanistan was neither possible nor desirable. The Taliban were enforcing a strict interpretation of Sharia law, with all that might mean: girls were forbidden from attending school, and had their opportunities to work drastically limited. There was a war against the arts, centred on a ban on the depiction of the human form, and including the destruction of cultural monuments. Most worryingly for the boy's family, which like ours was Hazara and Shia, the Taliban were conducting a harsh programme of discrimination – even massacres – against religious and ethnic minorities.

'I'm telling you this so that you understand,' said Halima. 'The boy's family cannot travel here to support him. We are doing a little to help. But the boy is basically on his own, here in Iran, without any financial means. I wonder how that fits with your criteria? Whether you still want to meet this boy?'

I told her that this was not important; for me, personality

and education mattered more. They – I think this may have come from my mother – suggested I might say no if he proposed, as had happened on previous occasions. No, I said, this time that would not happen.

'OK', said Halima. 'In that case, perhaps we will introduce you.'

I was still quite a shy girl at that time, and as I was sitting next to my mother I found the conversation embarrassing. So I tried to wrap it up by telling them that I was not yet thinking about getting married. *Of course you are*, they must have thought, but they diplomatically changed the subject to spare my blushes.

We returned from the trip, I went back to the university, and a year later, finished my semi-degree at Tehran University. It was a two-stage course for the full degree in radiation technologies, and I had been accepted at Tabriz University of Medical Sciences to complete the course there the following year. But despite the promise of an introduction, I had heard nothing from Mr Salehi since our visit to Mashhad the previous summer.

Then I was told that a four-day trip to Mashhad was being organised by Tehran University. Although I was no longer a student there, they agreed to put my name on a waiting list. I was so sure there would be cancellations that on the day I simply packed my case and went along and joined the queue, for all the world as though I had a ticket. Sure enough, others had dropped out, and I got my place on the trip.

I was determined to find Mr Salehi's house, to find out why he had not been in touch, and to discuss the option of the boy as a potential suitor. By this time I'd received other proposals of marriage, and had built up relations with other boys' families, so I needed an answer. When I knocked on the door, it was answered by a stranger. I said: 'Isn't this Mr Salehi's house?' The stranger looked slightly puzzled, and said: 'No, this is my house. Mr Salehi sold it to me.' I asked if there was any phone number or forwarding address, and the man said: 'No, we don't have any contact.'

He pushed the door shut, leaving me trembling and fighting back the impulse to cry. I was engulfed by sorrow, by the impotence that came of having lost something I had never had. Above all, I was so bitterly disappointed. It felt as though someone had poured a bucket of cold water over me.

7

The book you were after has arrived

'GOD THE HIGHEST will surely remove the sorrows of any sorrowful person who goes on pilgrimage to his shrine.'

The shrine referred to in this hadith from the Islamic Prophet is that of Imam Reza, at Mashhad. Over the centuries, religious buildings have sprung up around the Imam Reza mausoleum, including the huge Goharshad Mosque, four vast prayer halls, a library, a university, and four seminaries. Within the grounds are nine courtyards with fountains, pools and minarets, and a cemetery. It would take days to do justice to the museums alone, dedicated as they are to everything from postage stamps through calligraphy to carpets. The Mashhad complex, a city within a city, is a place to lose oneself in, the largest mosque in the world, and is the centre of Shia worship in Iran. It is thought to attract something like 25 million Shias annually.

This was where I took myself for prayers on that Friday. It was easy enough to find: I was soon caught up in the throng of worshippers on one of the city's tree-lined avenues, all bound for the mosque with its unmistakable blue and golden domes. I was very religious at that stage of my life, and believed that if my wish to meet Mr Salehi and the boy was so strong, it would be granted. A phrase went through my mind: 'If you are a believer, God will bring them to you.'

I crossed one of the marbled *basts*, or courtyards, to enter the great holy shrine, breathtaking with its intricate decorations of mirrors, gilt and tiles. It felt like being inside a jewel. Here there must have been three or four thousand people worshipping. I took my place among them, prayed, retired to a corner for some quiet time, and suddenly felt all the energy drain from my body. Quite exhausted, I curled up on the floor and fell asleep.

I don't know how long I slept. When I awoke, I opened my eyes and noticed somebody standing over me. I looked up to see it was Mrs Salehi, with her son. I was amazed. I told Mrs Salehi how I had wanted to find them, but didn't know how to, and had gone to the shrine not knowing what to do. Mrs Salehi said they had attended prayers, but when they tried to leave by the nearest gate, there had been such crowds in the shrine that they had been pressed in the opposite direction. The only reason they had found me was that they had been carried by the throng until they escaped into a space out of the flow of worshippers, which was where I lay. 'Now I know why the crowd pushed me this way,' Mrs Salehi said. I will never forget her words: 'It is meant to be.'

The next thing she told me was that the boy was 'still

available'. I put the two phrases together in my mind. The boy is still available. It is meant to be.

We went to the Salehis' new house, and they called the boy. He was not at his accommodation, so a message was left for the security staff to pass on: 'The book that you were after has arrived.' There was an invitation for him to come to the house for lunch the next day.

I was ready in good time, but he did not arrive. And so began the wait. Time has never passed so slowly. 'Don't worry, Shakar, I'm sure he will be here soon.' We waited, and waited, and still he did not come. I began to think he was not coming, that he did not want to meet me, that someone had said something to turn him against me…

It was not until mid-afternoon that there was a noise in the hall, and in he came, carrying a bag of grapes. 'So sorry! I have been at work. I only just got the message. I came as soon as I could!'

He was charming, smiling, wanting to talk and share the grapes and sit down all at once. I almost forgot that we did not already know each other, and laughed when Mr Salehi went through the motions of making a formal introduction. The boy's name was Ibrahim.

After tea, Mr Salehi stood up. 'OK, why don't we leave you two alone? I'm sure you have plenty to talk about.'

We did. Family, beliefs, education, all the big issues in life, all unpacked and paraded and compared. 'Do you feel psychologically ready to be married?' 'Do you?'

There was so much that needed to be said, so much we agreed on, it seemed too soon that Mr Salehi came back into the room. He smiled. 'You know, you've had three hours of chit-chat! Haven't you finished yet?'

It was time for me to go, as I had to get back to my accommodation. Mr Salehi saw me out, and asked what I thought. 'If he is what you say, and what he says, he is a good proposal.' We arranged to meet again at *Nowruz*. The start of the Persian new year, and coinciding with the vernal equinox, this is a night of traditional music, food and celebration. It felt auspicious.

But before that could happen, just two weeks later, I had taken my brother shopping in the bazaar back home in Tehran when we came face-to-face once again with Mr Salehi and Ibrahim. It was another purely chance encounter. 'It is meant to be,' I thought to myself once more.

Here, at last, was my opening to make things happen. I invited them home, where I told my parents: 'We have guests! Our old friend Mr Salehi, and a boy I don't know.' I felt sure my white lie would be forgiven. Mum served tea, and the conversation moved so quickly that before long Mr Salehi was discussing intentions with my dad. My father said: 'It is my daughter deciding these matters now; my opinion does not matter much, so let them talk to each other.'

Dad was being a little disingenuous here. Having quickly discovered that Ibrahim was known to his brother, as the families had once been neighbours, my dad found his opinion beginning to matter once again. After dinner, my mother and the menfolk – Dad, Mr Salehi and Ibrahim – set off to visit my uncle, who confirmed not only that Ibrahim was who he seemed to be, but that he was 'a good boy' from a decent family.

It must have been obvious to my father that this time there was a very real prospect of marriage, because the next step we took was at his suggestion: premarital screening tests. The idea of this may look like mistrust, but it is actually the norm in Iran, especially in circumstances such as ours where it had not been possible for our family to meet Ibrahim's.

The following morning we met and went to the hospital for the tests. The screening was to include DNA blood tests, considered essential in a country where consanguineous marriages between cousins are so common, since children of such marriages are at increased risk of genetic disease and congenital malformation. There were also tests for sexually transmitted diseases, and a drug test on Ibrahim, to make sure he was not addicted to any substances. We might not associate Iran with endemic drug problems, but opiate abuse here is three times the global average, the highest rate of any country in the world, partly due to the country's position as first stop on the substance transport route from the poppy fields of Afghanistan to Europe. Which is why tests such as those undertaken by Ibrahim were seen as nothing more than a sensible precaution.

When we left the hospital, we suddenly felt free. Just the two of us, nobody telling us what we should be doing, free to do what we liked and go where we pleased in the city. We went to the university bookshop, bought some textbooks, and I met a few friends who I introduced to Ibrahim. We stayed out all day. It was all so perfectly normal and extraordinary at the same time, to be with this new best friend who might soon be my husband. For now, we just had to be careful to adhere to the normal proprieties, taking particular care not to touch bodies when we travelled home in the minibus.

'Where have you been all this time?'

'Just... getting to know each other a little better.'

The test results were returned on the Thursday, with no

red flags raised. We went to the market and bought two rings: silver for Ibrahim, and gold for me. There was a celebratory lunch at our house, after which, punctually at 2pm, Mr Salehi asked us if we were all ready. He produced the marriage contract, and a pen, and we both signed.

The uncle and cousins were invited to this lunch, but there was still such antipathy that they did not come. Instead, Mum sent a traditional gift of sweets to them, and we heard later that they threw the sweets out into the corridor, as a token of disrespect.

Later, Ibrahim had to visit them to get permission for the marriage, the uncle standing in as proxy for one of Ibrahim's own family, as the person who knew him best. He returned looking shaken and explained that the cousins had made veiled threats. Dad told him he should be careful.

'You could get beaten. They might even kill you. Look out, and if I were you, I'd think about getting married very soon.'

After lunch, Ibrahim took my bags to the railway station. I had tickets to go to the new university at Tabriz on the five o'clock train, a twelve-hour journey. On the platform, at the end of these whirlwind few days, Ibrahim kissed me goodbye. He was going to stay in Tehran until the marriage certificate was sorted out.

This was a very strange experience: to have been single a week ago, then engaged, and now, it seemed, separated so soon. During the time we were apart, we wrote to each other often. I'm not sure I was very good at letting him know my feelings, but he was such a lovely letter writer, who opened his heart and soul to me. He even, as a gesture of the greatest confidence, sent me his diary to read. This was very candid, and contained revelations that you would think twice about making to anybody, and that I cannot repeat here. It seemed extraordinary to me that he was opening up his private, personal life to me – someone who was still little more than a stranger. It gave me tremendous faith in this amazing man.

Over the next year we met when we could. Ibrahim came to Tabriz, and stayed in a friend's room, while I slept in my university dormitory. The second night we rented a hotel room, but were very careful and didn't do anything that might jeopardise our future. After a week, he returned to Mashhad.

The next time, I visited him in Mashhad, without telling the family, to avoid any complications. We just needed to spend time together, even if it was only in a basic hostel. We talked about our future: I had a year to go at university, and Ibrahim had decided he wanted to take a masters.

Meanwhile, my parents continued trying to persuade us to get married sooner rather than later. We visited them in Tehran, and came away with very mixed feelings. Of course we were delighted to be getting married and wanted to be surrounded by friends, wanted all the world to be invited to share our happy day. But my mum and dad were still upset that the attitude of my uncle and aunt was putting such a spanner in the works. We didn't want our wonderful day to be spoilt with bad feelings, hostility, or bad words.

Nine months after we had signed the marriage contract, Ibrahim and I were married. It was an unusual event. Hazara weddings are steeped in tradition, with rites of passage before, during and after the ceremony itself, each of them a set piece in which costumes, flowers, various foods, books, mirrors, coins, rugs and so on play symbolic roles.

Our wedding would probably not have followed all of those traditions, and in ideal circumstances would have been closer to a simpler Afghan wedding. But on the day, there were no guests, and there was hardly any ceremony.

We had settled on this as – we hoped – a way of pouring oil on troubled waters. Our uncles and cousins would have made a fuss about refusing to come, and we didn't want to put the rest of the family in a position of having to take sides either with us or the uncles. So we invited nobody.

One of the traditions at a wedding is to sacrifice a lamb, and serve the cooked meat to the guests. We had a lamb, but no guests to eat it. So instead, my father distributed the meat raw. This was how many of the family first knew that we had got married. My father, so often a stickler for procedure, somehow seemed to prefer to do it this way. 'You are students; it was better for you to save your money, instead of wasting it on stupid ceremonies.'

It was, as I said, quite an unusual wedding. But I had got the husband I wanted.

8

In the wake of the Taliban

THERE WAS NO HONEYMOON. When the time came for us to leave, at the end of our brief wedding 'ceremony', I made my tearful farewells to my mum and dad, my brothers and sisters. Then Ibrahim and I lugged our two suitcases to Tehran railway station, and caught the train back to Tabriz.

It was the start of my final year at university. I was still in a room with three other students, but having got married I imagined the university would give us married couple's accommodation. It would be sufficient for us both, either to live here until I had finished my course, or until we found something more suitable. But on arriving at the university campus, we were told we were forbidden from using it as a married couple. According to Islamic rule, it is the responsibility of the man to provide accommodation and shelter. It is no good for the man to say: I have fulfilled my responsibility, by marrying a woman with accommodation.

'But we've just married! This is our wedding night!'

'And these are the rules.'

It was one anti-climax after another. We made some phone calls, Ibrahim got fixed up to stay with a couple of friends who were studying at the same university, and I retreated to my room.

We started searching for somewhere we could live together, and eventually found a basement studio flat – a small room with a kitchenette. We bought a piece of carpet and a cooker; all we could afford to make the flat liveable. Then we went to the market, and bought eggs, tomatoes and vegetables. Our first meal together was an omelette, which we ate sitting on the piece of carpet.

Ibrahim started working in a job friends had found for him, as a book keeper in a stone factory. With this new-found financial stability, and with thoughts of starting a family, we discussed the possibility of investing in a property of our own. In Iran, refugees could not own properties outright, any more than we were allowed cars of our own or, as mobile phones became more common, SIM cards. This remains the law, even now, although rich Afghans have always been able to get round it by asking their Iranian friends to buy proscribed goods in their own names. But we were allowed a semi-mortgage, which would give us a property for a fixed duration, after which the landlord would refund our deposit. I calculated that we could manage this by raising the substantial amount of capital with a student loan and by borrowing from the family. We managed to amass 700,000 tomans (to put this in perspective, Ibrahim was earning

35,000 tomans per month at the time). We found a suitable flat, and negotiated the deposit down from 1 million tomans to a figure we could afford.

Everything was going to plan, the paperwork signed, and we were waiting to be given a date when we could move in. But then there was some confusion with the estate agent. We were getting no replies to our enquiries. We tried phoning a few times, and found it impossible to get through. 'Only one thing for it,' said Ibrahim. We went round to the estate agent's office, to find it shut. Not just shut, but evidently abandoned.

We went to the police, who confirmed our worst suspicions: the estate agent was a swindler, who had a habit of collecting money from students, disappearing, and re-emerging some time later working under a different name. Each time he stuck around just long enough to cash a deposit, then vanished before the police could reach him.

In the aftermath, we had no cash, and survived on a subsistence diet of whatever was cheapest. We ate a lot of beans.

Meanwhile, I discovered I was pregnant. When I told my mum, she reminded me that traditionally grandparents make a gift of clothes for the first child. 'I've got a better idea!' I told her. 'Instead of clothing, do you think you could give me a sewing machine?' The machine cost Mum 1,200 Iranian toman, which would only have paid for one outfit of baby clothes. I bought a few metres of cotton cloth, some in baby blue and some in baby pink, and made two complete sets of baby clothes, which I embroidered with golden ducklings for good luck. I also made some baby bedding.

About this time, I sat my finals, and finished at university.

We had to decide what to do, whether it would be better to return to Tehran or Mashhad, where we would at least have a roof over our heads. Neither option was ideal, because there was still bad feeling in the family about what had happened with my marriage, and we worried that if we went back, the relatives would interfere. So we stayed, and moved into cheap accommodation – an old house built in the traditional way with clay walls and a wooden roof. I was in early pregnancy and feeling very sick, but luckily my sister Hakima had her school summer holidays and came to look after me. She didn't know much about cooking, so fed me lots of yoghurt soup.

We were overjoyed when the five-month scan showed a healthy baby. They told me it was a boy, so I named him Sina, after Ibn Sina (known in the West as Avicenna) the great Afghan polymath. Not only was Ibn Sina highly significant as a physician, astronomer and philosopher of the Islamic Golden Age, but he is regarded as the father of early modern medicine.

At seven months, though, the scan showed the baby to be a girl! I decided to name her Sara. Living in Iran had made me aware that my own full name is difficult to pronounce, and because we were refugees with an unknown future, I wanted my children to have simple names that would fit in, in whatever country they might find themselves.

Towards the end of my pregnancy, my mum came to look after me. It was a mild February day, a Friday, that my waters broke and Mum took me to St Zahra's Hospital. Ibrahim was not allowed to come with us, because in Iran men are banned from attending childbirth. So I called one of my friends, who was doing a midwifery placement in Tabriz

Medical University, and she came to support me, and even helped to deliver our lovely baby, Sara. I had met this friend during registration, when we were amazed to discover we both shared the same name, surname and year of birth! Given how few people from Afghanistan there were at the university, this was quite a coincidence.

The following day, Ibrahim came to take me and Sara home in a taxi. When we came out of hospital, it was snowing heavily and the town was already covered with a surprising depth of snow. It snowed so much that the hallway in our house collapsed. So my mum took Sara and me back to her house in Tehran until Ibrahim found us somewhere better. We struck lucky: not only was our new accommodation closer to where Ibrahim was working, but Ms Rana, the landlady, was wonderful with babies, filling the role of a grandmother. I have to confess Sara was a difficult baby, but Ms Rana helped in many practical ways, such as getting Sara bathed. I found it very touching when she brought gifts for Sara's first tooth, usually a tradition for family members.

A lot happened during the course of my pregnancy. Like many millions of people around the world, we watched the television with horror as the events of Tuesday, 11 September, 2001, unfolded. Again and again, the amateur footage of the grotesque moments of impact of two aircraft, on the North and South Towers of the World Trade Center, were repeated on TV, and each time was no less shocking, no more comprehensible.

As we soon learnt, this was the deadliest terrorist attack in history, introducing an obscene new methodology: hijacking airliners in mid-flight to be used as guided missiles. The only precedent we could think of for such an attack out of the blue was Pearl Harbour, but this time we didn't even know who was declaring war on whom. None of us could guess what might happen next, but we all understood that nothing was ever going to be the same again.

Over the coming days and weeks, the consequences for the USA started to be made apparent. The death toll, the injuries, the psychological damage; the monumental clean-up operation; the economic costs of damage to infrastructure and property; the new security measures. But before any of these came the clamour for justice.

The attacks had been carried out by members of an Islamic extremist network whose name would shortly become globally infamous: al-Qaeda. This was the brainchild of a rich Saudi, Osama bin Laden, who had travelled to Afghanistan to volunteer in the early years of the Soviet-Afghan conflict. Bin Laden saw this as a holy war in the Islamic cause. He became one of the sponsors of the mujahideen, supporting them with arms and funds, and bringing in and training Islamist fighters from other Arab countries.

By 1988, it was becoming clear that the war against the Soviets would be won. The sense of impending success prompted some of the foreign mujahideen into planning tactical support for Islamist struggles elsewhere, such as Palestine and Kashmir. A number of interrelated organisations were formed to implement this, including al-Qaeda under Osama bin Laden.

The following year, as the war ended with the withdrawal of Soviet forces, bin Laden returned to Saudi Arabia as a hero. Over the next eight years, at first in Saudi and then Sudan, he developed his manifesto, including the proclamation that a Christian-Jewish alliance, led by the United States, was conspiring to fight and destroy Islam; and that secular laws should cede to a strict form of Islamic religious law, sharia, perceived as divine decree.

In 1997, bin Laden established a new base in Afghanistan, by now under Taliban rule. Soon after, he issued two fatwas, calling for a cessation of American involvement in the Middle East, and proclaiming that Muslims had a duty of jihad, to attack Americans until the grievances were reversed. He initiated a series of terrorist bombings, including the 1998 US embassy bombings. Out of this would come 9/11.

American reaction to the terrorist attacks was to launch a 'war on terror', which sought to undermine militant Islamic extremism. Intelligence indicated that the Taliban were giving al-Qaeda a safe base of operations in Afghanistan, and it was resolved that the best way to expose al-Qaeda was to remove its cover, by taking down the Taliban government. America and her allies unveiled Operation Enduring Freedom just three weeks after 9/11, and achieved the dramatic success of driving the Taliban from power within the following two months. In December 2001, the Bonn Conference established a new governmental regime, the Afghan Interim Administration, under the leadership of Hamid Karzai.

We followed every twist and turn. Was Afghanistan really being held to blame for 9/11? Would yet another war in our country solve anything? Could the Americans succeed where the Russians had failed? There was such a history of the imposition of leadership – and such a dearth of negotiation – in Afghanistan's past that it seemed doomed to lurch from one seizure of power to the next, with no investment in infrastructure or long-term strategy. No evolution, only revolution.

But then, after the birth of Sara, it suddenly struck us.

Here we were, Ibrahim and I, newly educationally qualified, married, householders and parents. In other words, responsible, useful people. And there was Afghanistan, with the Taliban recently ousted, heralding the start of a time of optimism, when the country could be put back on its feet. But it was going to take more than Western investment. The ranks of a new infrastructure would need to be filled with educated professionals, and they could only come from outside the country.

'People like us!'

We had both always wanted to return to the country of our birth, where we could be among our own people, and serve our community best. If it were ever to happen, now was the time.

First, though, there was the question of my university tuition fees. Every student who graduated in Iran was expected to work for the government, for twice the time they had spent studying, in lieu of repayment of university fees. But there was a Catch 22: as refugees, we were not permitted to work for the government. We were still trying to figure out how we might resolve this impasse, when I went to the university to collect my diploma. There I was told I would be expected to work at an Iranian hospital for eight years. When I revealed that our plans were to return to Afghanistan, they told me that in that case, I would have to repay 300,000 tomans in tuition fees.

At that time, the average monthly wage was 35,000 tomans. Savings – and family money – would not come close to raising the levy. But there was one possible avenue of assistance: as refugees, we might be eligible for a grant from the UNHCR. I petitioned them for help with the funds, explaining that I had gained my degree as an Afghan refugee in Iran, and now I wanted to use it to help my own country.

It took nearly a year to sort out, and while our application was going through the system, we returned to Tehran. My dad was then working in an iron factory, and he managed to secure Ibrahim a place at the works. After a while, Ibrahim moved to another job, working in a clothes-dyeing factory.

One step at a time, the UNHCR confirmed that our petition was legitimate and within their scope; did some background checks on both of us; and informed us that they would be making an offer. When at last the formal notice of grant arrived, we checked down to the bottom of the page, and there it was: 200,000 tomans! It was two-thirds of what we needed, tantalisingly close. We totted up our own savings, got on the phone to all and sundry, and found we could raise the balance in donations and loans from families and relatives.

Ibrahim returned to Afghanistan first, alone, to search for work before Sara and I joined him. Because we were not sure if it would be safe in Afghanistan, and thought Ibrahim might have to return to Iran, I kept his residence permit. So he crossed the border with no ID, introducing himself as a stateless Afghan. This raised suspicions and he was taken by the police for interrogation. I spoke to him afterwards on the phone.

'What happened? Were you hurt?'

'They were rough. I guess you could say it was torture. They were suspicious because I was educated but had no ID, so I didn't fit the categories. That made me a nuisance. So they wanted to intimidate me, to teach me a lesson.'

In the meantime, while we had been waiting to clear my university debt, a neighbour had called. She had been invited to attend a wedding the next day, but didn't have a suitable jacket to wear. Her tailor was busy, and it was short notice to find an alternative. Did I know anybody who could help?

'I could do it. I know how to make clothes!' It was one of the homespun activities I had pursued while still at school, to help raise funds for my further education.

I measured her up, worked overnight and had something ready to show her in the morning.

'But this is wonderful, Shakar! You are better than my tailor!'

She came back with a friend, and a proposition: if I could make clothes for some of the local women, they would look after Sara for me. It was a good arrangement, and worked well for all of us. My new customers said they preferred me, as most of the tailors were men, and I had a better understanding of women's needs.

In the spring of 2004, I got the go-ahead from Ibrahim to join him in Afghanistan. It was only at this stage that I discovered the scale of repatriation of Afghans from Iran. Over the previous year, more than 400,000 of us had taken the decision to return, and the UNHCR was playing a key role in the massive logistical exercise. For example, there was the question of Afghan refugees' contracts with Iranian landlords to be sorted out. I went before a committee in Tehran, formed of members of the UNHCR, Afghans and Iranians. They told my landlord that he would have to return the deposit we had paid, and that if he didn't have the money he would have to raise it by selling the house. This of course made him very angry, and he went out muttering curses on us all. When he had gone, the committee calmly told me that they actually had no power, and what they had told him was only a threat. But it worked! We got our deposit back.

When the time came, I was sorry to say goodbye to so many friends and family, and to be leaving the country where I had grown up. I had very mixed feelings, and could only hope that we were doing the right thing. Then Sara and I went to the local repatriation centre, with our allowance of two pieces of luggage. We got on one of the free UNHCR coaches, and set off in a small convoy out into the mountains and the deserts – the landscape of my childhood.

We crossed the border at Dogharoun, where UNHCR representatives were supplying returnees with the means of restarting the lives they had left behind. Some got shelter-building kits, some working tools, some food aid. They checked on how I had been making a living, and gave me money and a sewing machine.

I looked round, and suddenly there was Ibrahim. We had our faces covered, against the strong wind and the blowing sand, and we both laughed at nature kicking up such a fuss, like a stroppy kid trying to spoil everybody's fun. It wasn't going to bother us! The wind and the sand blew us into each other's arms. We were so happy to see one another; and sad at all we had left behind.

9

Wrong sex,
wrong ethnicity,
wrong religion

MOMENTARILY, I SAW MYSELF once again as that vulnerable six-year-old who, twenty-one years earlier, had landed in a foreign country not knowing what the future would hold. Then, I was with my parents; now, I had a family of my own. And this time, of course, I was back in the country of my birth. But that country was almost as precarious as when we had left. Would it welcome me back, as one of its own? I was returning, after all, as an uprooted person; and I knew that uprooted people can be allowed to take nothing for granted. In fact, one of the first things we did on arrival was to have our names added to the electoral register, and collect our voting cards, as if to cement our individual identities with that of our nation.

It had cost a lot for us even to set foot in this UNHCR

transit camp, just on the Afghanistan frontier. The financial and mental burdens of extricating ourselves from our obligations in Iran were one thing. What was harder was having to say goodbye to friends and neighbours. When would we see them again?

We decided to make our first base in the oasis city of Herat. This would be convenient in more ways than one: Herat sits in the north-west corner of Afghanistan, and the main road into the interior from Dogharoun takes you directly there, following the valley of the great Hari Rud, sometimes called the Herat River. It's a straight run of just 100km, along what is now the Islam Qala – Herat Highway. The road is perhaps better known by a more ancient and romantic designation, as it forms one of the main arteries of the great network of trade routes known collectively as the Silk Road. Herat stands at one of the historic crossroads, where not only merchandise but culture too – from the Middle East, India and Central Asia – come together. The cosmopolitan character of the city has earned it a reputation for colour and broadmindedness.

What's more, this is where Ibrahim's parents were living. They were originally from the same Afghan province as my parents, and in fact we had all migrated to Iran at the same time. They had returned to Afghanistan much earlier than us, back in 1995, and were drawn to Herat by its proximity to Iran and the sanctuary that country offered if life in Afghanistan became difficult again.

We found quite an enclave of people from our own background building up in the city. My uncle, aunt and younger cousin had returned from Iran one year before us (the elder cousin stayed in Iran), and they too had settled in Herat, where they had built a house. Then we arrived, and at much the same time my mum and dad turned up, with all of my brothers and sisters except my oldest brother, Mohammad Baqer, who had gone to work in Greece. We all got together, and there were tears of joy and laughter when we met Ibrahim's parents for the first time, and introduced them to their beautiful new granddaughter Sara. Then there were the introductions to the rest of the family, and to all the friends, and the neighbours... Our first few days were a whirlwind of faces and houses and endless cups of tea.

My parents stayed with my uncle when they arrived in the city, and quickly made the decision that this was where they intended to settle. They were keen to have a house of their own as soon as possible, and the easiest way to achieve this in Afghanistan is to build from scratch. Within the first month, they used all their savings to buy a building plot, a small piece of land of about sixty square metres. I drew up a blueprint of sorts, a layout of all the rooms, trying to get all the spaces in proportion and creating a natural dynamic for the way the rooms were to function. My father gave this his approval, and I could tell he was pleased about my plan and excited to start work on a house of his own.

Before we knew it, we were all making cement blocks to build their house. This snowballed when other relatives who had returned at the same time as us saw what we were doing, and found that the layout of my mum and dad's house would suit them too. Soon, a whole row of identical houses was being built. My parents' neighbour was my cousin, the next house was her husband's sister, and so it went on. In the end it became a settlement of mostly Hazara people, with a name of its own: Jebrael.

We were welcomed so generously it made me feel Herat would be a lovely place to live. I quickly applied for a job in the radiology department of Herat Regional Hospital, and was offered a post. But when it came to finding work for Ibrahim, it was a different story. There was no shortage of vacancies, but every time Ibrahim applied for a job, his ethnicity worked against him. The way he was spoken to, the negative attitudes, the dismissive body language, all sent out a very clear message: Hazara boy, no thank you.

So after one month, we decided to turn our backs on the 'broadmindedness' of Herat, and try our luck in the anonymity of the capital city, Kabul. We had two lovebirds, that were our pets, which we reluctantly left behind with Ibrahim's parents. We tried not to dwell on the symbolism of the lovebirds, and what this separation might portend. We wanted only good omens.

We stayed for the first few weeks in the house of a close childhood friend of Ibrahim, Rashid Mohammadi, who shared his one room with us, and lent us futons and duvets. After this, we rented a small, bare room in the Kabul suburbs, which we fitted out with the most basic essentials: carpet, pressure cooker and picnic stove. Enough to survive on.

It took six months, but Ibrahim did manage to find a good job in Kabul, at the Ministry of Financial Affairs. Even here he was treated with suspicion and as a second-class employee, not being given any office space for the first month, but having to stand behind other people to do his work.

I applied for a job at Kabul Medical University as a lecturer, but found the application process a very long one. In the meantime, I heard a report on the TV at Mr Mohammadi's house about a new CT scanner which had just been acquired by a clinic in Kabul. Intrigued, I went to the clinic, showed them my credentials, and offered my services to operate the scanner. I got the job, but on what I thought was a lamentably low wage for a skilled job, of between thirty and fifty dollars per month, depending on the workload. As the rent on our room was fifty dollars per month, this left me with precisely nothing over. By the time Ibrahim started earning – a similar wage to mine, enough to pay for our upkeep – we had burnt through our savings.

Our poverty meant that, for example, we could only afford one coat for Sara, at a cost of five dollars. So I would have to wash it at night and hang it over the fireplace to be dry for the morning when I took her to the nursery. Fortunately for us, every organisation in Afghanistan has a nursery, so mums can take their children to work.

Also this year, I voted in a national election for the first time. These were in fact the first democratic elections held in my country since before I was born, the last having been a parliamentary ballot in 1969. This time we were voting for a new president for Afghanistan. It was busy at the polling station, where we were given ballot papers showing the name and a photograph of each candidate. When we had voted, we had to dip a thumb in ink, to counter any 'vote early, vote often' fraud. The election attracted a large turnout of around 75%, despite rumours of intimidation, which we did not witness. It was even arranged by the International Organisation for Migration that over two million Afghan refugees in Iran and Pakistan could participate. The most popular candidate, Hamid Karzai, had been installed as Interim President of the Afghan Transitional Administration back in 2002. Now standing as an independent in a field of eighteen candidates, he won with a landslide 55% of the vote. He was popular at home, was seen as a moderating force, and perhaps most importantly had a great rapport with Western leaders.

After a long, drawn-out vetting procedure, my application for the post at Kabul Medical University was accepted. This came as a great relief to me, as it meant I could give up the job as CT scanner operator at the clinic. Professionally, I could tell that this was a second-rate operation, which was brought home to me when I found the director, a medical practitioner, trying to interpret scans by comparing them with images in a textbook.

But this was not the reason I was so desperate to leave the clinic: the fact was that I had been on the receiving end of repeated attempted sexual assault by its director. Even though he had two wives, he was still trying to sexually abuse his female employees. When he tried to touch me, I threatened him that I would immediately leave his clinic if it happened again. This was about the strongest sanction available to me, as I knew that reporting sexual predation to the authorities would get me nowhere, and would only invite further harm to me. After this, I kept my distance from him. It was a weight off my shoulders when the job offer came through from the KMU, and I could hand in my notice at the clinic and put all that unpleasantness behind me.

By the time I started work at KMU, I was seven months pregnant. This meant that after I had been working for only a month, I went on maternity leave. A few weeks later, we were blessed with the arrival of a second daughter, a sister to Sara, whom we named Zahra.

Having set my foot in the door at KMU, I applied for

a post in a scientific cadre position. My qualifications and experience suited me perfectly to the job. But what I hadn't bargained for was the institutionalised attitudes of the university administration.

Firstly, I went through endless hurdles of being asked for more and more supporting documentation. All my documents were in order, so in the end they changed tack and told me I would need to sit a cadre exam. But at the end of three months of study, they discovered that I was the only person in the country with my qualification, so there was nobody to examine me. I was advised instead to take the same exam as a radiologist. I would be examined on just one book. The only trouble was, the single available copy of that book was in the university library, and as I was not a lecturer, I was barred access.

I appealed to the chancellor of the university, telling him this was a crazy situation. He agreed, and wrote an order to the library. They gave me the book to photocopy. When I had a chance to examine it, I found it was written in old Persian, which is a Dari dialect, and with half the terminologies in Arabic and English – none of it was in modern Persian. I had to underline all the words I did not understand and ask for help in translation from a colleague. At that time, of course, there was no access to Google or the internet.

I took the exam and did well, despite having been able to study for only a very short time. The chancellor came to my help, sitting in on the exams and asking the questions at the viva voce examination. I answered all the questions correctly, and they signed my application for acceptance in the scientific cadre.

At this stage I was thrown once more on the mercy of

university admin, who continued to make many problems for me, in their zeal to find the one faulty document, the one flaw in my application, that would disqualify me. As I later realised, they were deliberately making my life difficult, as a ploy for getting me sent back. In their eyes, I was 'the wrong sex, wrong ethnicity, and wrong religion'. The application process, which normally took other people two months, was dragged out in my case to nine months. Eventually the phone call came through: 'Your approval letter is ready for collection,' I was told, 'and don't forget to bring some sweets.' So on my way to the university office, I called into a sweet shop and picked an attractive box of *gaz*, the Iranian nougat made with pistachio, almond kernels and rose-water. That should do the trick, I thought! But when I formally presented it to the man at the counter, he opened the box, glanced at the sweets, then stared me in the face. I have never seen an expression of such contempt. 'These are not the sort of sweets I meant', he said. Silly me! The sort of sweeteners he wanted were made of printed paper, not nougat, and came not in a box but a bundle. I suppose everything would have gone more smoothly if I had resorted to bribery, but it was against my principles, and it would have robbed me of my sense of achievement to have been accepted on the strength of a backhander, rather than on my own merit.

I ended up working for Kabul Medical University in the radiology department. This was another eye-opener. About a year into my work the KMU scientific committee referred a paper to me for peer review, written by the head of the physics department. He was very definitely old school, with his long beard and habit of deferential fussiness, with much bending of his head to show respect. When I read his paper,

I immediately realised it was not written in an acceptable way for publication. I had to teach him – even though he was two ranks higher than me – how to use evidence-based references. I ended up rewording much of the paper, which went on to be published in his name.

Soon after I had started at KMU, I was asked if I would be interested in working on a university collaborative project with the French Medical Institute for Mothers and Children (FMIC). This 169-bed training and referral hospital was set up through an innovative four-way partnership between the governments of Afghanistan and France, the Aga Khan Development Network and a French NGO called La Chaîne de l'Espoir. Managed by the Aga Khan University, it was at the forefront of efforts to reconstruct Afghanistan's healthcare system. They needed a supervisor in the radiology department, which was running a project to make MRI and CT scans publicly available. When they phoned me to say I had got the job, I was still on maternity leave, and I had to tell them that my baby Zahra was only thirty days old, too young for the nursery to accept. I thought that might be the end of it, but they said: 'Don't worry, we will put a cot in your office!' So I started working at FMIC, sometimes holding my baby in my arms, while operating the CT scanner and at the same time teaching radiographers.

I worked there full-time for two years, and after that, part-time, juggling this with my work at the Kabul Medical University.

The hospital was brand new and still getting established, and I found that not all the staff in those early days knew what they were doing. I was told that radiographers and radiologists from France would be visiting to train operators and doctors, but it seemed to me that the sooner the hospital was functioning properly the better. So I started a course to train my colleagues in radiology from scratch, on a curriculum agreed with the university chancellor and my boss at FMIC. It went well, saw fourteen radiographers qualify, and helped towards a new enthusiastic mood in the radiology department. But it must have annoyed the head of department, who regarded me as a rival and began undermining my position. I wasn't consulted on issues central to my work, and found that decisions were being made behind my back. I was given all the rubbish jobs, such as marking essays, while those members of the faculty fortunate enough to have been born of the correct gender, or ethnicity, or religious persuasion – better still, all three – shared among themselves the prestigious responsibilities, such as delivering lectures. It made me so stressed that I began to develop stomach pains. Why was I putting up with all this? Surely I would do better to simply get out, to go back to education, take an MSc, maybe even a PhD. I would stand a much better chance at landing a higher-level job that way, than I would by trying to work my way up through this corrupt system.

In September 2005 I found myself heading back to the polling station. Not for another president, but this time for the governing councils: the Wolesi Jirga (Council of People, or House of Representatives), the Meshrano Jirga (Council of Elders, or Senate), and local councils. What was so significant about this election – what excited me, as an Afghan woman – was that nearly half of us casting ballots were women. In the lower house, sixty-eight out of 249 seats were set aside for female members, and in the Senate, twenty-three out of 102. In our patriarchal society, this was an unprecedented advance towards equality.

Meanwhile, the radiology department had been asked to help re-establish the Kabul Cancer Centre. Radiology treatment worldwide comes under the auspices of the International Atomic Energy Agency (IAEA), and as their stipulations had not been met during the Taliban reign, the Centre's credentials had been lost and it was closed down. And since the Taliban had been ousted, the IAEA had introduced in 2004 a new Programme of Action for Cancer Therapy (PACT), whose stated aims are to 'respond to the needs of developing countries to establish, to improve, or to expand radiotherapy treatment programs'. An application to re-establish the cancer centre under PACT conditions had been made to the IAEA, I learned, in 2005, but nothing seemed to have come of it.

I volunteered to help the head of department in instigating the re-establishment. This was in 2007-2008. My first job was to send an introductory letter to the International Atomic Energy Agency, and I received a very long letter in reply. They informed me that the application made in 2005 had resulted in two responses: a budget had been allocated, and a list drawn up of which things should be done by which deadline. The letter detailed each of those bullet-points, and noted that not a single one of the items on the list had happened.

To address all the specified work to get the project started, I had to take the relevant file out of the archive of the Ministry of Foreign Affairs. I discovered that, in what I am sure was an instance of racism, the file copy of my original introductory letter had been torn into shreds by one of the civil servants. But because it was an official letter, they had had to take it back and stick all the pieces together to deposit it in the archive.

Not long after, my head of department suffered a heart attack, which meant he was unable to continue work, and he even had to leave the country to seek medical aid. That left only one person able to lead the project for the re-establishment of the Cancer Centre in Kabul. Me.

10

No! No!

'MY DAUGHTER, I AM ILL. I am in pain, I am bleeding, I do not know what is wrong with me. Please, I need you to come to me.'

It was 2008. Dad was calling me from Herat, where he and Mum were still living. As soon as I rang off, instinct kicked in. I phoned Ibrahim to ask him to book me a ticket on the next available flight, and to look after the girls while I was away. Then I went to the airport, straight from work, and boarded the Kam Air Boeing 737. Little more than an hour later, we were touching down in Herat.

I found my father in a poor state, not only bleeding but with infections. He had not received any adequate medical treatment. What could I do? Just when I was feeling I had landed in an impossible situation, I remembered a colleague who ran a private clinic in Herat. I gave him a call, and arranged an urgent consultation.

The blood count suggested what I had suspected – that Dad was suffering from leukaemia. But because of the crazy state of healthcare in the country at that time, although he could get diagnosed in Herat, he could not be treated: there was no oncologist. Not in Herat, not anywhere in the country. I did some research, and found the only place offering the treatment he needed was in Pakistan.

Ibrahim and I took him there. It was a horrible journey of eight hours, which took us right the way across Afghanistan. The first section, from Herat to Kabul, was not so bad, but from there to Jalalabad, we had to follow the Mahipar Road, a narrow highway with countless hairpin bends above sheer precipices, considered to be one of the most dangerous roads in the world. The further we went, the worse it got. Beyond Jalalabad, the road remained dangerous, narrow, bumpy and dusty.

We crossed into Pakistan via the famous – or perhaps infamous – Khyber Pass, where the road threads its way between the tribal lands of Pashtun overlords, where smuggling is rife and travellers always at risk of gunmen extorting levies for 'safe' passage. We had enough anxieties already, over my father's health, and all the way through the pass I rehearsed terrible scenarios in my head, then tried to formulate ways of dealing with them. Fortunately we came through unscathed, but by the time we reached our destination, the city of Peshawar, we were all shaken and exhausted.

They were expecting us at the clinic. First, the oncologist needed to know as much as possible about Dad's medical background, and I had to answer most of the questions on his behalf, partly because of the language barrier – the conversation was in English – but also because Dad was too weak to concentrate. Then the consultant put Dad, very gently and caringly, through a simple physical examination. All done, he scanned his notes, then turned to me and said: 'You would do better to take him home alive.' I looked at him, not comprehending what he was saying. Was Dad going to die if we stayed here? But then I understood. He meant that Dad might not be able to withstand any treatment he could offer. He was going to die soon, and it was better for him to do so with dignity, and at home with his family.

But – I wanted to shout – we were here to get him treated! It was my duty, both as a daughter and as a medical professional, to give him the best chance of prolonging his life. We might not be able to stop the cancer, but surely we could slow its spread. Whatever it took, that had to be the priority.

So we went through the blood tests, the bone marrow test, and in the end the oncologist prescribed a course of chemotherapy. Dad would need a programme of medication given at regular intervals over the next two months. It was very expensive. But it was a no-brainer. We got the prescription, and as soon as the medication was available for collection we got in the car to drive back, not to Herat but to Kabul, where I could look after him.

He complained that he would not survive the journey. I could sympathise with him, as it had crossed my mind that neither of us might complete the horrendous drive to Peshawar, and now we had the same misery to go through again to get home. Dad was in such a frail state that the travelling must have been a real physical challenge to his system. At one stage, he talked about dreaming that his mother was taking him home, and he seemed almost to welcome the prospect of eternal rest. It was such a relief that we made it, back to our house in Kabul, with Dad still alive and in one piece.

It was about a week later that I phoned my mum in Herat, and told her she really needed to be with us. And she was to bring Zahra with her: we had tried Zahra at the nursery in Kabul, but she wasn't having it. She hated it so much that there was no point in us insisting that she go there 'for her own good' when it was clear that all she got from the nursery was distress. It was difficult to know what to do, with both of us working and dependent on childcare, but eventually we had settled on the best alternative: she went to Herat to live with my parents. She was happy there, got plenty of attention, and it was fun for her to be cosseted by her grandparents. In turn, she brought sunshine into their lives, and a new sense of purpose. They doted on her.

Since I had picked Dad up, he had been missing Zahra very much. The first time he showed any signs of his old animated self since we had left Herat was when I told him the news that Mum and my daughter would be travelling to join us in Kabul. He carefully lowered himself onto a seat, and despite the pain his face radiated happiness. 'My Zahra is coming!'

But he knew the number of his days on earth was limited, and it was instructive how he spent some of that time, making sure he had paid his bills and was leaving his finances in good order. He spoke of the 'one regret', that he would not survive to see his children's weddings, as at that time I was the only one married. But he told me that he had written into his will a codicil that after his death, he wanted me to be in charge of family affairs. 'Especially where your sisters are concerned! It will be your responsibility to ensure they marry appropriately.'

This remit went beyond simple approval. As I said to Dad, women in our society don't have much by way of constitutional rights, but their lot can be greatly improved by having additional rights written into the marriage contract. So I would tell my sisters to write down everything they would like to see stipulated in the agreement. Obvious examples would be rights of divorce, children's custody, work, and education. There might be binding rulings on the consequences of the man taking another wife, having an affair, or behaving badly. It would be my duty to help my sisters get the best guarantees for their married lives.

Dad was getting perilously short of breath. All the next night I barely slept, waking up whenever his breathing became more laboured, worried that his fragile body could not stand the effort of all that wheezing. Worried even more that it would stop.

The following morning I took him to the hospital. Leukaemia causes an imbalance in the blood cells, something the body is not well equipped to fight against. The simplest way of remedying deteriorating blood quality is by a transplant. We had already had a consultation about matching blood types – his blood group is AB+ – and discovered that a doctor friend, Dr Amin Hamedi, head of a hospital in Kabul, was of the same group. He had volunteered to donate blood himself. I called him from the hospital, and to my amazement he dropped everything from his busy schedule and came straight to the hospital. All the necessary equipment – blood pressure cuff, needle, tubes, blood bag and so on – were quickly assembled, and within minutes Dad was receiving a transfusion of untainted blood.

We took a taxi back home. But there was an unforeseen snag: because of the awkward topography outside the house – an alleyway running from the front door to the street – the taxi was unable to draw up outside. And by now, Dad could not walk. What to do? My scientific mind could find no solution. And my imaginative mind was even less use, seeing this as a kind of allegory, in which that innocuous alleyway in front of the house was one of those mortal hurdles that are sent to test us. Solve the riddle and Dad's life would continue; fail, and accept the inevitable consequences.

Ibrahim had a much less fanciful way of tackling the problem. He gently lifted Dad onto his back, carried him through the door, and lowered him onto his bed.

After the journey, Dad was confused, not knowing, for example, what time of day it was. I asked him if he would prefer to return to Herat. I thought he would be more comfortable at home, and it was important that he should be surrounded by as many members of his family as possible. He had no other relations in Kabul, nothing else to keep him, now all his medication was sorted out. 'Yes. Yes, that is what I want.' So Ibrahim booked tickets for all of us to travel to Herat – including my mum and Zahra, who had only just arrived from there – and ordered a taxi to take us to the airport.

But all this activity had been too much for Dad. Coming in from the taxi he was gasping 'No, no!', and it appeared that, despite all our cares, he had been jostled while being lifted. For anybody else this would not have signified, but as the doctor told us, Dad's blood vessels were very frail and easily broken. It seems likely that some blood vessels, probably in the lungs, ruptured. Dad was more confused than ever, and very short of breath.

I asked Ibrahim to call a good friend, Mr Rezayee, an elderly man who lived just a couple of minutes away, to talk to Dad. I think it was some comfort for Dad to hear that familiar old voice. He asked the friend to recite some verses of the Qur'an which relate to getting healed. Dad started to join in with the recital, but after a little while his voice grew quieter, and finally petered out. We realised he had lost the ability to talk.

We took him outside for some fresh air, to a raised patio area, with a mattress on the floor, where he would be more comfortable. It was there, with the rest of us standing close by, gathered all around him, that Dad breathed his last and passed away.

Not much later, my older cousin, Mohammad Hussein, phoned from Iran to ask how he was doing. 'Your uncle is absolutely fine now. He is in no pain.' The cousin understood.

In our society it is important that the dead are buried as a matter of urgency. One of my work colleagues from FMIC, Mr Sadeqi, wanted to come and visit my dad, so I asked him to bring a winding bandage with him, for the initial preparation of the body. Ibrahim went out to order a coffin, to get some ice, because the weather was so hot, to put father in the coffin, to pack the ice around him. All done, he called the airport, to make the necessary changes to our tickets. Poor Ibrahim! The day was 22 May, his birthday.

Strangely, we all slept well that night. We were mournful, of course, and there were tears. But Dad was free from his agony at last, and a profound peace had descended on the house.

We flew to Herat with the coffin, where the burial service was held with all the family and relatives in attendance. My younger cousin Mohammad Hassan, who was then living in the city, came with his family, as did my mother- and father-in-law, and all the more distant relatives living in Herat.

In our mourning rituals, we regard days one, three, seven and forty as auspicious. There were too many other obligations, of work particularly, for us to observe the full forty days in Herat, but we stayed and paid our due respects for seven days of lamentation, before returning to Kabul. On the fortieth day, those in Herat gathered at Dad's house, while the rest of us read passages from the Qur'an, and shared condolences, where necessary by phone.

It made me think how much Dad meant to me, how similar we were in our obstinacy and determination, how painful our differences felt. I think we were so close as to feel that there should be no conflicts between us, and when we fell out over a difference of opinion, we were both distraught. We each felt offended that the other should not entirely agree with us, and at the same time we had the greatest respect for each other's point of view. The internal conflict this caused was distressing for us both. I thought back on the terrible time when my father refused to speak to me. I know that he was as upset as I was, and my only regret is that we could not resolve it sooner. I cherish the moment when he accepted me as his loving daughter once again.

But for all my prayers, I lost my father to cancer. I was devastated. And, at the same time, I was hopeful that the path I had chosen might at least help others in their fight against this dreadful disease.

11

The Kabul Cancer Centre

I KNEW I HAD TO ACT FAST if there was to be any chance of the IAEA taking seriously the proposal of getting a radiology centre in Kabul up and running. Everything the university had presented up to now must have looked to them so amateurish, ill-informed, confused and entirely lacking in urgency. There was no way they would approve a licence unless the team and the infrastructure were up to speed.

We arranged an expert mission, so that representatives of the IAEA could meet us, discuss our needs, and inspect for themselves the existing set-up. When the first experts flew in from Iran, I collected them from the airport in a taxi, and took them to their hotel. A couple of days later another expert arrived, this time from Hungary. Over the course of a few days the team came together, and at last we set up a preliminary security briefing at the United Nations office in central Kabul. I was on tenterhooks, wanting to see what sort of sense they could make out of the muddied history of the attempts to re-establish a cancer centre in Kabul. What would their priorities be? Of one thing I was sure: they would leave me in no doubt as to what I was up against.

One major issue, it turned out, was recruitment. Candidates had been proposed by the university, but at interview the shortlist failed to impress the experts. They were concerned that the applicants were middle-aged, and not great at speaking English. They were all professionals, each with their own field of expertise – surgery, internal medicine and so on – but this only raised further questions. Why would these people want to change discipline, if their careers were on track? It didn't seem to make sense, when a move to the cancer centre would be at best on the same level, rather than a step up. Everyone deserves a fair chance, of course, but I couldn't help wondering if cronyism was at work behind some of these nominations, and the vacant posts were perhaps being seen as sinecures. When the interviews were done, the experts laid out their priorities. What they wanted to see was dynamic, flexible, enquiring minds. Young motivated people with fewer family restrictions would be ideal. Fresh blood. Not what they had seen so far.

I put this not entirely Afghan-centric critique to the chancellor of the university. 'Of course, we must respect our colleagues,' he said, 'but the experts are absolutely right.' We went through the records and he began to nominate medical graduates from recent years, high achievers with marks over 75%, who were fluent in English. An all-star line-up! We assembled a new team of fourteen candidates in all:

myself and a colleague, each with a BSc degree in radiation technologies, another colleague with a BSc degree in physics, seven doctors, three radiographers and one nurse.

I collected all of their CVs to include in the submission I was preparing for the IAEA. As I was getting the paperwork ready to send off, I realised there were some big gaps in our proposal. Our minds had been focused on the core intervention: external beam radiation therapy. But what about brachytherapy, the use of implanted radiation 'seeds' placed within or next to the tumour? That would have to be part of the programme, but we hadn't discussed it. And there would need to be a diagnostic centre, too, beside the oncology and treatment centre. We had a round-table meeting, drafted auxiliary proposals, one for the brachytherapy and one for the diagnostic centre and, at last, sent it off.

It took a year before we received a reply from the IAEA – a year that I spent in a state of high anxiety. What if our proposal was accepted, but with impossible conditions? Or worse still, we were rejected outright? Eventually, I checked my inbox and there it was – an email from the IAEA. We'd done it! It was an immensely proud moment to learn that the proposal had been accepted. We were given a start date of 2010, and told we would be eligible for funding totalling $1.3 million.

The email also contained information about training. They told me I would need a masters if I were to function as project leader. There was not the expertise in Afghanistan for our training to come under the aegis of a domestic university, so the IAEA had recommended institutions abroad. The most convenient of these – the nearest to home – was in India, so that became our first choice, and in due course we had our training programme accepted for accreditation by one of the medical institutes in Uttar Pradesh.

Right away I started preparing for our year in India. I sorted out appropriate clothes, bought some shawls to wear when the weather got colder, and made lists of everything I would need. But the months went past, and we heard nothing from India. Other vocational opportunities came up at Kabul University, which friends were able to apply for but I was not, because they knew I had signed up for the IAEA and Uttar Pradesh. It became a joke among my friends, to ask if I was going to apply for the latest tempting opportunity, and then say: 'Oh no, of course, you're going to India! When exactly did you say you were going, Shakar?'

I put up with that for two years, with Indian bureaucracy prevailing and no sign of a start. Eventually, at the end of 2009, I put in a complaint to the IAEA about the slow progress, and asked if they could change the host country for the trainees, as we were getting nowhere with India.

There was an additional cause for anxiety. There had been a resurgence in Taliban terrorist attacks, and if the country reverted to all-out civil war, the future of the cancer centre would be even more in jeopardy. There were currently 37,000 US troops in the country, tasked not only with countering the Taliban, but disrupting al-Qaeda, and stemming the flow of foreign fighters over the Afghan-Pakistan border, all while protecting themselves. There were surely not enough foreign troops to accomplish this massive set of tasks without assistance, and the Afghan government didn't seem capable of managing effective security forces of its own. Who would keep the streets of Kabul safe?

For a long time, right up until early July 2010, I heard

nothing from the IAEA. We were close to the deadline for starting, and I was beginning to think my MSc would never happen. Then, out of the blue, came an email. The IAEA had accepted my request, and said that, instead of India, candidates would need to travel to the UK. We were told to sign up for the medical physics course at the University of Surrey, at a place called Guildford, in England. Oh, and did we mention this before? To get on the course, I would need a Higher English Certificate.

It meant that I would have to sit an examination called the International English Language Testing System, or IELTS. If I passed, I would be awarded a certificate of competence, proving my ability to use routine written and spoken English at work or for study. This is a gold standard, recognised by many universities and employers, as well as the UK Home Office for visa applications.

Could I pass? I had studied English language at school in Iran, where it is mandatory from Year 7 up. I loved English, loved the English teacher, Mrs Beigi, and finished high school with a good grade. Then, when we returned to Afghanistan, I worked with some English-speaking colleagues at the French Institute and had to generate reports and communicate in English. So I felt quite confident. But when I started preparing for the exam, I remembered that when listening to BBC radio, I could understand only two or three words from each sentence because of the accent. The English I had learned was American English.

The course at Surrey was due to start in September, so I had very little time to prepare – less than three months. As a desperate measure, I took one month's leave from the university, likewise from the French Institute, where I was still working part-time, to cram up on English. In one of the numerous bookshops in Pul-e-Surkh, I picked up some English textbooks, and a six-volume book of study exercises with sample exams and CDs. Next, I sent in my application to sit the exam. Then I shut myself in at home, put my head down, and braced myself for a month of intense study sessions of sixteen hours a day. After a few days I gauged my efforts with some trial exam questions, and found I was far from good enough. I took to carrying my books and cassette player with me into the kitchen, into the bathroom – everywhere I went. I would select a word in English and think about how to use it in a sentence. I could not afford to waste a minute.

At the end of the first week, I heard that my uncle in Herat was very ill, and was asking to see me. I did what I had to do, travelling there and taking him to see a doctor. He was suffering from a chronic lung disorder, and had already had one lung removed while living in Iran. Bronchitis was preventing the other lung from functioning well, and he could not breathe properly without oxygen. So we went to the market, and bought a huge oxygen cylinder. We had it delivered and set him up with a face mask, but even when he was hooked up he was struggling. I was with him for two weeks, staying awake to look after him in the night. Then, knowing I had done all I could, I gave my cousin and other family members advice on how to care for the poor man, and returned to Kabul.

I had been able to continue some of my English cramming while I was in Herat, but back in the capital, fearing I had fallen behind with my language studies, I looked for an English tutorial class. There was one! But it was on the far side of the city, some two hours travel from our house. I attended a trial course of three sessions, and picked up some very useful tips in exam techniques. But at the end of those three days I was fed up with having wasted so much time sitting in Kabul traffic. Surely I could do better on my own? It was getting towards the deadline of my exam, and the results I was achieving from trial tests gave me hope that I might manage a pass.

The IELTS exam comprises four tests, each contributing 25% of the total marks. The four papers cover reading, writing, listening and speaking. On the day, I discovered I had a problem affecting my hearing, and in the listening exam could hear only buzzing. It felt as though my ears were blocked. I raised my hand and asked if I could be given headphones, but was refused because 'headphones can only be issued by prior request'. I came out of the exam room convinced I had failed.

You might expect each paper to be marked, for simplicity, out of ten, or twenty, or one hundred. For some inexplicable reason, this particular exam is scored out of nine. The pass mark for each module is six, and I needed to gain a pass in each module, together with an aggregate score of at least 6.5. When the results came in, I found my score in the listening exam was a fail of five points. How I achieved any points at all in listening I am still not sure.

I contacted the University of Surrey, explaining that on the day of the exam I must have had a head cold which affected my hearing. Understandably enough, they told me this was not an adequate excuse for waiving the English certificate condition of my offer. My place was still secured, but I would have to resit the exam.

Time was getting very tight indeed, so I applied straightaway to sit the next available exam, which would be held one month later, towards the end of August. I just hoped this would give me enough time: they wanted me to submit my English certificate by September, the course was due to start on 1 October, and there was to be a one-week induction before the start of term. Before that, I had to get to Britain; and before that, I needed to obtain a valid UK visa.

At the second exam they were ready for me, with a pair of headphones sitting prominently on my exam desk. Everything went according to plan this time, and I passed in all subjects.

As soon as the results came in, I applied for my visa. Not a visa for the UK, but for India. This was for the simple reason that it was not possible to obtain a UK visa in Afghanistan. So although there were direct flights to Britain, they were no good for us. Our only way to make the journey was to fly to India, apply there for a UK visa, and once it came through to get on a plane to London.

So absorbed had I been in all this that I hadn't been giving much thought to my family. It took Ibrahim to remind me. 'Your sister, Masumeh, is getting married. You know what that means for us?' Masumeh was by then twenty-seven years old, with a degree in psychology, and working as a teacher in a primary school. Her wedding ceremony had been set for 14 September. And what Ibrahim was referring to – what it meant for us – was an enactment of the obligations to family that had been set out in my dad's will. Not only to make sure she married appropriately – that was all taken care of – but also to host the ceremony in our house. So for a few days, we had a great throng of guests – uncles, aunts and cousins, parents-in-law, sisters and brothers, even my brother Mohammad Baqer who came back from Spain, where he had been living for many years – filling every space in our house, getting ready for the ceremony.

I hadn't told my family much, if anything at all, about my plans. It had been such a whirlwind, and the intensive studying made me put social duties to the back of my mind. But Zahra did the job for me. One evening she had been lying with her head on my lap when she abruptly got up, crossed the room and lay down with her head on my aunt's lap. 'Mummy's going to the UK,' she announced.

This kicked up quite a sandstorm. 'Why are you going? On what date do you plan to leave us? And for precisely how long, Shakardokht, do you propose to be away?'

So, at last, it all came out. When I'd explained everything, there was a discussion about practicalities, which I'd perhaps not given enough attention to until that moment. Now you are leaving, who is going to take me to the specialist for my abdominal pain? And have you even thought about what will happen to your family? Who do you suppose is going to care for your children?'

I think Zahra must have instinctively known this was a conversation that urgently needed to happen. The sandstorm blew itself out, with a happy ending. 'Why don't I come to live in your house, for the year you're away? You'd like that, wouldn't you, Zahra?' Mum: always there when needed!

There was a further building-block to the security of the family I was leaving behind. Ibrahim's career had taken off, as he had recently succeeded in securing a job in the second vice president's office, a very good job, well paid, with his own driver. This came as a comfort to me, making me think that my year away from home was not going to put the family into such peril after all.

There were lots of hugs and tears when the time came to bid farewell not only to my mum and my sisters and brothers, but to my two little girls too. Then I left the wedding ceremony, which was still ongoing, and Ibrahim escorted me to the airport, where I met up with two other students who had passed at the same time as me, Musa and Qasem. We were all heading for the University of Surrey, and we all knew this would not be a straightforward journey.

We flew first the relatively short hop of two hours to New Delhi. There we took a taxi to the city centre, then headed a little way out to the diplomatic enclave of Chanakyapuri, where we soon found ourselves on the steps of the British High Commission. Armed with our passports, our English certificates, and our letters of acceptance from the University of Surrey, we filled out our applications for UK student visas, which would be valid for up to fifteen months. They would take, we were informed, up to four weeks to process. 'Time to enjoy yourselves, in our beautiful city! Is this your first time in India?'

We just hoped there were not going to be difficulties with the visas. At the airport, Musa had let on to us that there was a discrepancy in his graduation certificate: the date of birth it showed did not match that in his passport, which was given in the English calendar. Such problems are common in Afghanistan, where the date of birth is not regarded as significant. So, often, in documents such as graduation certificates, Afghans will put their Persian date of birth. Sometimes only the year of birth is known, in which case a random date is often used. Not surprisingly, many Afghan people have difficulties when they try to go abroad and are found to have discrepancies in their documents. I advised Musa to take the risk, in the hope that nobody would notice.

We booked into a fairly cheap 3-star hotel with self-catering, to cut down on expenses. I came to regret this: I had a bad experience of bed bugs in the hotel, developed a skin allergy, and couldn't sleep during the last few days of my stay. In the end, I took to leaving the light on to deter the bugs. But we tried to make the most of our time, including a sightseeing tour of the Taj Mahal, organised by the hotel. A few days later, Qasem began to complain that he wasn't feeling well, and needed to rest from our sightseeing schedule. He quickly fell quite badly ill. He had contracted dengue fever, a vector-borne illness related to malaria, most likely picked up from mosquitos in the throng at the Taj Mahal. His symptoms were typical of the disease: a high temperature, headache, muscle and joint pain, nausea, loss of appetite and a rash. There's no treatment; you just have to sit it out and hope for the best. I spent the rest of our time in the beautiful city of New Delhi not sightseeing, but nursing.

Fortunately, Qasem's symptoms began to ebb after the second week, but he was still recovering on 30 September – the day before we were due to start at Surrey – when a call came through. 'Your visa is ready for collection.' The three of us nearly fell over ourselves, rushing to the High Commission, and then straight to the airport. Not a moment to spare! We had already missed fresher week, and were really worried that we might miss the entire course if we did not sign on in time.

At the airline ticket desk, we asked excitedly for 'three single tickets to London, please!'

But when we were going through security, Qasem was stopped. His visa, it transpired, was faulty. Not the UK visa but the visa on which he had arrived in India. It failed to state that he was in transit to the UK from India, and the only way he could get round the bureaucracy was to comply with the conditions of his Indian visa by returning to Afghanistan, and then flying out to the UK from Kabul.

This was very unfortunate. Qasem had certainly recovered well enough to take the flight, but the after-effects of the disease made the stress of having his schedule interrupted a much harder blow to take. He decided to spend another day in India, sorting out a refund, before travelling on to Kabul. We just hoped and prayed he would be fit enough to manage all that on his own. He saw us off at the entrance to the departure lounge. 'See you in the UK!' Then the two of us headed for our gate.

12

Four in a bedsit

OUR ARRIVAL IN THE UK passed in a blur of jet lag, and all we could think about was following to the letter the instructions the university had given us for our arrival: how we should get National Express tickets, where we should board the coach from Heathrow to Woking, how to change for the train to Guildford. All the way I sat glued to the window, taking in the unreal, Technicolor lush greenness of the English countryside. And everything was so clean! It was not until some years later that I heard on the radio a performance of 'Jerusalem', and remembered vividly my first impressions when I heard the words 'England's green and pleasant land'.

The University of Surrey is a campus, sitting on the lower slopes of the hill which carries the red-brick cuboids of Guildford Cathedral, and facing across the river and railway line to the town itself. We found it an easy walk from the train station, still following the meticulous instructions ('Leave the station by the Guildford Park Road exit') the university had emailed us in advance. The care and attention that had gone into those notes represented to me the greatest of all the distinctions between the UK and my home country. We do not share the custom of indiscriminately lifting the burden from the shoulders of fellow beings in need of help.

We soon located our rooms. Duvets and pillows, we discovered, could be bought from the accommodation office. Then, with memories of other moving-in rituals, we headed to the nearest supermarket, on an expedition for cooking pots and pans and groceries.

Musa, I should have said, had previously suffered an unexplained paralysis, curiously reminiscent of the affliction my sister Hakima had suffered at the age of nine, which left him with a limp, and a weak hand and foot on one side. This had come home to me when we arrived, and I had to carry up the stairs not only my own bags but Musa's too. And now, as we were walking off the campus and I saw the supermarket signboard and read it aloud – 'Tesco' – Musa instantly retorted: 'I can't walk faster than this, even if you kill me.' I burst into laughter, because the sound of *tesco* in our local Persian dialect means 'hurry up'!

Our days in Afghanistan always start at six o'clock, and – despite the jet lag – that was the time we awoke from our first night in England. We got ourselves prepared, and at seven o'clock stepped out onto the campus. There was nobody to be seen.

We didn't know what to do with ourselves, so we hung around in the corridor of the physics block, waiting for somebody to come to our rescue. Eventually, at about 9am, a man in a lab coat walked in. 'Hi. I think I know who you are. I'm John Williams, radiation lab technician. Come and meet the team.' He took us upstairs to the admin office where there were handshakes all round, the room echoing with 'hello, hello, hello'. Then on with the formalities, of getting booked in and being given our schedules and log-in codes. 'Is it just the two of you?' We explained how our other colleague had been obliged to travel back to Kabul, and would be joining us later.

During our induction, the course director, Professor David Bradley, picked me as international students' course representative and that was a great experience for me. When later I asked him why he had picked me, he said that he was looking for someone with enthusiasm, and that was what he saw when he looked me in the eye.

A week later a familiar face appeared around the door. Hey! Qasem! We were so happy that the three of us were reunited; that the gang was whole again. With all of us away from home and family, it seemed a good plan to make our own social bubble. We agreed to cook together, study together, go to the library together and make our own study group. We were often working into the small hours of the morning, always aware of needing to put in that extra effort to overcome the disadvantage of not having English as our first language. I found that under exam conditions, I had to translate each question in my head and prepare the answer in Persian, translate it into English and write it up. The extra time this required meant that I never managed to get all the answers written within the limited time.

Pooling resources helped us all, as one of us – Musa – had

a background in pure physics and a good understanding of nuclear physics and radiation science, whereas Qasem and I both had backgrounds of studying radiation technology in Iran, as well as biology and medical science. Later, we got into conversation with some other students from Saudi Arabia, who said they'd noticed us working together. 'Perhaps you could show us how a study group works?' We invited them to join our group.

I think my two colleagues and I were all aware of the danger that our decision to work in a bubble risked social exclusion, so in our first month at the university we went to the welcome party of the Friends International charity. Friends International is an evangelical support group for international students in the UK and Ireland, which offers access to British culture while spreading the message of Christianity. All three of us were very wary of religious groups, but decided to trust Friends International because they were endorsed by the university.

As it turned out, many of the people we met became good friends. A couple called Paul and Fran invited us all for Sunday lunch, and although Musa was reluctant, Qasem and I accepted the invitation. We had a very warm welcome, and they even served us halal food. That was the first of many Sundays with Paul and Fran and their guests.

It was extraordinary how many lasting friendships I made through Friends International, and how much kindness I experienced among people who helped us, gave us lifts, invited us to events and went walking with us.

Before Musa, Qasem and I sat the exams, we had a discussion about how we were feeling. The three of us all admitted to having quite low confidence levels, partly because of the language barrier, but more because we were unsure that the university teaching we had received in Iran or Afghanistan came up to the standards of Western universities. When the results came through, we found that of the 47 in our class, 23 had failed. This didn't look good for us, and there was a nail-biting moment before we got our individual results. Musa, Qasem and I were amazed to learn that we had all passed with distinction.

This was not the result I would have expected. I called in to the course director's office. 'How come half of the class are native speakers, and we have had all these fails, when at the same time some of us non-native speakers have had such good results?'

'Well, the thing is', he suggested, 'you have learned academic English, following approved courses, but some of the other students were taught by their parents, and what they speak is – for our purposes – the wrong English!'

During my MSc year, I was still employed as project leader for the re-establishment of the cancer centre in Kabul, and had been working on the project plan for the proposal that had been accepted by the IAEA. They had sent me preparatory material explaining how to complete a project plan, in the form of a training CD and some booklets. This was when I realised that the whole project was in danger of unravelling if I did not personally take back control. With a little background digging, I discovered that communications that came in to the Kabul project from the IAEA, for example, invitations for site visits to similar projects abroad, were being channelled through government departments in Kabul, and used as perks for unrelated officials to take freebie foreign trips. So instead of me, somebody from the

Ministry of Foreign Affairs had participated in a seminar on how to prepare the project plan, while I had only received the CD and booklets.

My colleagues from the MSc course came to my assistance in preparing the project plan, and funnily enough, out of eight project plans that the country submitted that year, ours was the only one that reached the required standard. Other projects, even those whose taskforce had attended the preparatory courses, failed to have their plans accepted.

After graduation, I realised that none of us had gained enough clinical experience to feel confident at the thought of being thrown in at the deep end of working as medical physicists, straight from the MSc course. I expressed this in a meeting with the IAEA, and persuaded them to set up clinical placements for us. They chose, apparently at random, a university hospital in Turkey.

At this point came an offer, 'something for you to think about', from the University of Surrey. Would I like to stay on and study for a PhD?

As if life wasn't complicated enough already!

I didn't know what to do. On the one hand, I had the commitment to go back to Afghanistan: Ibrahim and the girls and the house were all waiting for me, and my heart was set on seeing through the re-establishment of the cancer centre. On the other hand... Gaining a PhD could be a game-changer. I called Ibrahim to ask him what he thought. He took on board the pros and cons of my dilemma before bringing a new factor into play: he said that his job in the Afghan government gave him an insider's view on how the political situation was playing out. From what he had seen, things were not going so well in the country.

This came as news to me. I hadn't had time to follow developments back home very closely over the past year, but what I had heard sounded quite positive. Since I had been away, the headlines suggested that the incoming US President, Barack Obama, had a proactive attitude towards Afghanistan, and was determined to get its problems sorted. He had a new strategy, to escalate the Afghan mission with an additional 30,000 personnel, on top of the 68,000 by then in place. They would train and work alongside Afghan security forces, creating the conditions for the United States to transfer responsibility for security to the Afghan government.

The other big news, which had broken a month or two before I spoke to Ibrahim, was the demise of Osama bin Laden, killed in the successful US hit-squad raid on the compound in Abbottabad, Pakistan, where he and his family were holed up. This was seen as a major success on many levels. It was a boost to US morale, satisfying the popular thirst for revenge; was a propaganda coup for US intelligence; and a blow to al-Qaeda. All of these factors seemed to me to strike a positive tone for the future of our country.

'Yes, it does look like that,' began Ibrahim, 'and that is what everyone wants to believe. But what people inside government are saying is much less optimistic.' For a start, he explained, there was growing concern about Pakistan's position. Bin Laden's safe haven in the country must have been sanctioned from a high level, and that was symptomatic of Pakistan's slippery stance on Islamic terrorism. It was futile for the US to attempt to sanitise the terrorist threat inside Afghanistan when insurgency missions could be carried out from across the border, where the US had no redress. As for the death of Bin Laden, what difference would it make on the ground? Among al-Qaeda and Taliban militias, he would be seen as either a martyr or an irrelevance.

'OK,' I replied, 'but what about Barack Obama's new strategy? What about all those extra troops?'

This was met with another 'Ah, yes, well, but' from Ibrahim. Obama, it appeared, had been pushed into a corner: a huge percentage of Americans no longer supported the war, fearing another Vietnam, and US politicians on both sides were demanding a substantial withdrawal of forces from Afghanistan. So Obama had compromised, putting a time-frame for the drawdown of the additional troops deployed in what was being called 'the surge'. They would start being sent home in a year's time, July 2011, with the first 10,000 standing down by the end of the year, and a further 23,000 by the summer of 2012.

'When this was announced at work, a kind of groan went through the building,' Ibrahim told me.

'Because it shows the Americans are not really committed?' I asked.

'No, not that,' Ibrahim replied. Some of the people he worked with had an army background, and they'd explained that in a conflict, the one thing you never do is give advance notice of a withdrawal.

'The Taliban are not stupid. They will use this to their advantage. They can afford to sit and wait. And then the country will become a more dangerous place.'

He relaxed his tone. 'There are so many things like that happening, and none of it looks good. Maybe it's a good idea to change your plans to return to Kabul. I'm wondering if you might do better to go for the PhD?'

We worked out that we could afford it, because the offer from the University of Surrey came with an overseas student scholarship, which covered the cost difference between home and overseas student fees. At that time home students were charged £4,000, whereas overseas students had to pay £14,000. The grant would cover the £10,000 shortfall.

I called the chancellor of Kabul Medical University to explain the situation, and he said he was happy for me to pursue the PhD, and he would send me a letter of consent. There was, inevitably, a struggle with the Afghan Ministry of Higher Education, who wanted to know how I could have accepted the offer without going through its channels. I explained that this scholarship was given not to a government, to be awarded through open competition, but to an individual: it was specific to the University of Surrey's patronage of me as one of its students, and was non-transferrable. It took some arguing, but eventually I got written consent to take a three-year sabbatical.

There was one other matter I needed to finalise: what would happen to the clinical placement as part of my MSc, which was to be funded by the IAEA, and had been agreed with Turkey?

I called the IAEA: would I be able to complete the placement in the UK, while working on my PhD? They told me that if I could find a position in a hospital where they would charge no more than £6,300 for a placement fee, then it was doable. So I asked one of the lecturers, Professor Andrew Nisbet, who happened to be head of medical physics at Royal Surrey County Hospital, if he could help me with a placement. He told me that if I drafted a placement plan, he would match the placement fee to that agreed with the hospital in Turkey. He counter-signed the plan, we submitted it, and the placement was duly accepted by the IAEA.

So, with placement at the Royal Surrey County Hospital and PhD at the University of Surrey both secured, I began my second year in the UK. I hoped and prayed that Ibrahim's prediction would prove wrong. It was my ambition to return to Kabul and resume work on the re-establishment of the cancer centre.

My PhD project was placed under the principal supervision of Professor Nicholas Spyrou, with Professor David Bradley, who had been my MSc course director, as secondary supervisor. The PhD would continue my MSc research, which had been into a particular application of radiotherapy for the treatment of cancer. One of the dangers with this form of therapy is that there may be toxic side-effects including damage to, or even the death of, healthy cells and tissues adjacent to the tumour. This can occur if the dosage is too high, or not delivered precisely on target. The obvious remedy of reducing the radiation intensity can, paradoxically, cause further problems: too low a dosage can cause the tumour cells to become resistant, so that more intense radiation is needed, which may in turn cause further damage.

The challenge is to find a way of maximising the proportion of radiation collecting in tumour tissues, while minimising its spread to normal tissues. Researchers have investigated a number of different ways of working towards this ideal. These include an ongoing search for the perfect method of measuring and directing delivery, while strategies have been developed for lowering the radiation resistance of tumour tissues, and enhancing the tolerance of normal tissues.

The work I was involved in followed yet another path of investigation: finding ways of making the tumour tissue itself more sensitive to radiation. We were looking at achieving this through implanted radiosensitisers – chemical or biological compounds whose presence in cancer cells may enhance the effective dose of radiotherapy. My area of research involved the application of nanomaterials – metallic elements with a high atomic number. It has been found that elements such as bismuth, tungsten, silver and gold have an ability to increase the deposition of radiation: in fact these 'nanoenhancers' may have up to 100 times greater absorption coefficients than soft tissues. It was exciting to be involved in this because the science was young, and I hoped my research would add to its pool of knowledge.

When I first came to England, I was sure I was doing the best thing for myself and for my family. It was the last thing I wanted, of course, to have to spend time away from Ibrahim and our daughters, and only by taking the long view, of eventual benefits promising to outweigh immediate hardship, could I go through with it. As it was, everything seemed to be going according to plan during the year of my masters, when we all kept happily in touch with regular phone calls.

So it came as a great shock when I went home on a trip to Afghanistan during the Easter holidays in 2011, and saw how badly my absence had affected Zahra. She had lost so much weight that she was literally just bone and skin. My mum told me she had become very fussy about food and wasn't eating well. It was upsetting to see, and I couldn't help thinking it was my fault, and I began to beat myself up for being neglectful. I tried to explain the situation to Zahra, but she was of an age when she needed her mum and no amount of explanation could take that away.

At the end of my trip, I found it very difficult to have to leave my children again, with nothing resolved on how to improve Zahra's state of mind and health. But I had to return, to finish my course. I resolved to phone home more frequently, so that at least Zahra would be able to hear my voice regularly, but whenever I phoned, she was crying: 'Mummy, when are you coming back home?' Our phone calls were usually about an hour in length, and each time Zahra would be sobbing from start to finish. When I put the phone down, I had to try to switch off my mind, forget about Zahra and focus on my studies, especially as it was coming up to exam time. And although I knew that this was what I had to do, it still felt like the hardest, most unnatural, most unmotherly thing in the world.

Ibrahim and I discussed the situation, endlessly, every time we spoke on the phone. We both knew there was only one solution. On 20 October 2011, the vicious circle was broken when Ibrahim and the children came over to join me in England.

For this to happen, we had to have a UK family visa, which has conditions attached that are more exacting than my student visa. In particular, we had to prove that we had either sufficient income, or a substantial pot of savings, exceeding the particular bar set for our family group of two adults and two children. As Ibrahim had no proof of income, we were unable to qualify on the earnings stipulation, so the only way we could do it was to show a very healthy bank balance. Just one problem: we didn't have much in the bank.

Here, my colleagues Musa and Qasem came to the

rescue. They had graduated and were going on to Turkey to complete the IAEA clinical placement before returning home. They made us an incredibly generous offer, doing something which most people would hesitate to do, even for members of their own family: they deposited all their savings into my account in the UK, so that I had enough funds to qualify for the family visa. When it came through, I was able to return the money to their Afghan bank accounts.

While we were waiting for the family visa to be granted, Ibrahim had time to look into his own prospects for employment in the UK, and before leaving Kabul it was suggested that there would be a job waiting for him at the Afghan Embassy in London. It was a good job, which would bring in sufficient income for us to finance ourselves while my studies were continuing.

First, of course, came the convoluted process of Ibrahim and the girls getting to the UK, beginning with the obligatory stay in India. I advised Ibrahim to rent a short-term flat – a clean one to avoid the problems I had had with bed bugs. He had to rent the flat for a month, but the visa came through unexpectedly quickly, in just a week. Ibrahim had been so unsure about getting the visa that he hadn't actually handed in his notice at work in Kabul, and had to go back there to formalise his termination of employment. Meanwhile, I booked their ticket via Bahrain with Gulf Air.

One of my wonderful friends offered to take me to the airport. This was Ruth, whom I had met at the Friends International welcome party. I had been talking to Qasem when Ruth came up to me. 'Are you two speaking Persian?' she had asked. I said, 'Yes, how do you know?' She told me that her daughter Judie was taking a Persian language degree. I offered Judie some speaking practice, and we ended up having Christmas lunch with Ruth and her family. Ruth had become another good friend to whom I knew I could turn for help.

Ibrahim's flight was supposed to land mid-afternoon, but he phoned me in the night to say that in Bahrain they had been put onto an earlier flight. 'So what time will you arrive?' I asked. 'Er, it's going to be 5am.'

I called Ruth, full of apologies, but amazingly she was still happy to get me to the airport, to my eternal gratitude.

We were waiting in the arrivals hall, when suddenly I spotted Ibrahim coming through the door, pulling the luggage trolley, with Zahra sitting on one of the bags and Sara walking beside him. The girls and I all started crying, out of sheer joy and the sense of all of that pain from the past year in an instant swept from us. Ruth told me later that she had brought her camera to take some pictures but was so emotional herself that she couldn't do it.

The downside was that after Ibrahim had arrived, the embassy job that had been dangled before him was abruptly withdrawn, and someone else took the post. We are in no doubt this was corruption in action. It was so typical of the way Afghan bureaucracy operates: it's not who you know, but how much you're prepared to bribe them.

So, having arrived with great prospects, Ibrahim found himself jobless. He didn't have very good English, which made it more difficult for him to get work. The money I was bringing in gave us so little that we struggled to make ends meet. For our first two years as a family in England, the four of us had to live above a dry cleaners in the Guildford suburbs, in a cramped one-bedroom flat. Even this was beyond our means, so we turned the living room into a bedsit, which we rented out to another student. I couldn't help smiling. It had been sixteen years since I had enrolled at university, and since then I seemed to have come so far. Yet here I was, once again, living the life of a first-year student.

13

Like beads from the market

EVERYTHING WAS HAPPENING all at once.

Our family – Ibrahim, our daughters and me – were back together, at last. I was about to launch my PhD project into the use of nanoparticles as radiation sensitisers. And at the same time, I had been accepted for an IAEA-sponsored placement. If I tried to postpone that, I might lose it entirely. So I made the decision to start my PhD, and the placement, both at the same time as getting my family settled in their new country. The autumn of 2011 was to prove a turning point in my life.

For my placement, which was at the Royal Surrey County Hospital, I was given a role working on an NHS-wide assessment of the treatment of lung cancer, with a view to improving its effectiveness. The particular treatment I was assigned to look at was called 'stereotactic ablative body radiation therapy' (SABR). This is most often used in the destruction – 'ablation' – of small, well-defined tumours. What makes it different from most radiotherapy is that it uses many small, thin beams of low-intensity radiation. These are directed from different angles (that's what 'stereotactic' means), converging on the tumour. Thus the tumour itself gets a high total dose of radiation from multiple sources, while surrounding healthy tissue receives only the lower dosage of individual beams, reducing the risk of damage.

How do we know how much radiation is hitting the tumour? Research over the years has come up with a variety of ways of measuring this, and part of my job was to look at the limitations of the different methods. The problem was that while detectors such as diodes could be used on patients with simple treatment plans, there was nothing that worked for the more complex treatments like SABR. Instead, we tested the accuracy of delivery on a 'phantom', using a radiation-sensitive protein powder called L-alanine. It was not practical to carry out these tests on the patients themselves because the powder is very sensitive to temperature and humidity, both of which can vary wildly from patient to patient.

These deficiencies prompted me to start looking into the challenge of measuring accurately the actual radiation dosage. And the more I looked into it, the more it bothered me. I was concerned that we might end up with a detector that would pass the test for this particular audit, but might be impractical in other clinical settings for measuring the accuracy of the treatment of patients with lung or other types of cancer.

A question formed itself in my mind: what if you could

find a detector that would cover the whole range of dosage? One that was so small that many of them could be placed inside the patient's body, to tell us precisely how much dosage was delivered?

I began to find this question such a distraction that I decided to put my PhD on hold, to consider my options. I was already beginning to have doubts about my choice of PhD subject on the use of nanoparticles, which was not within my supervisor's main field of expertise. I contacted professors at UCL, who were themselves eminent in that field, and they told me they would be happy to come in as part of a supervisory collaboration. But Surrey made it clear that this was not going to work for them. Discouraged, I began to think of how I might find a way out of the predicament.

I took my concerns to Professor Andrew Nisbet, who had helped secure my placement, and asked if he had any alternative PhD projects. He suggested I might be interested in doing something related to my placement experience, by switching to a thesis relating to SABR technique. There was plenty to be done in this area, he told me, because at the time SABR was still new to the UK, and treatment centres were just coming on-line with commissioning. Professor Nisbet wanted me to look at the optimisation – ways of guaranteeing the best outcome of any SABR therapy – and proposed Dr Catharine Clark, Consultant Clinical Scientist in Radiotherapy at the Royal Surrey, as co-supervisor.

Catharine invited me for a meeting, when she made a great suggestion: what if I spend a couple of weeks looking into the optimisation, to see if it might be something I would be happy to pursue at PhD level? If I liked what I saw, she would talk officially to the university.

During those two weeks, I investigated the challenges and limitations of SABR. More than that, I thought about my own abilities and knowledge, to weigh up which areas I would be most effective at working on. I found my curiosity roused by the challenge of 'dosimetry', the ways of measuring accurately the amount of radiation reaching the target area. So I did some research, reading up on the relevant literature from the past ten years, and was thrilled to discover that my instincts were right: radiation detection seemed to dovetail with where my own strengths lay, promising the sort of career I had envisaged for myself.

So when the two weeks were up, I met again with Andy and Catharine. They looked at me apprehensively. Catharine spoke first: 'So, how did you get on with your investigations?'

'Well…' I wanted to keep them guessing, but couldn't keep up the pretence. 'Great! I'm very happy working on SABR – I'm excited by all the challenges it has raised in my mind – oh, and I feel it's a much better subject for my PhD.' Smiles all round!

But changing track was not so straightforward. My principal supervisor, Professor Nicholas Spyrou, thought I should continue my work on nanoparticles. I responded by sharing my core belief: I wanted to be involved in a project that would make me an expert in a clinical area, rather than on the theoretical side of medical physics. Nanoparticles, I argued, were not in a state to be used in the field. From the work I had already pursued, I realised that all I would undertake in this domain would be simulation and laboratory experiments, which interested me less. Medical science, for me, was not a pursuit in itself, but something with a defined target: to improve life outcomes. And that could only occur in a clinical setting.

Professor Spyrou generously accepted my explanation. It might not have been his own preference, but he recognised that there was no point in him insisting on something I had set my heart against.

There was also an issue about funding. The scholarship I had received was an Overseas Research Scholarship, awarded on the basis of the proposal I had submitted for research into the use of nanoparticles as radiation sensitisers. It would be difficult to present a convincing reason for abandoning the whole basis of the original award, and I risked losing the scholarship. The only way round it was to have my initial supervisors, Professors Spyrou and Bradley, and my new supervisors, Dr Clark and Professor Nisbet, working together as a directorial team.

Which is how I ended up with four supervisors! My fourth guardian angel, David Bradley, Professor of Radiation and Medical Physics at the University of Surrey, was an expert with ten years' experience of working on the use of optical fibres as dosimetry detectors. These had achieved very good results at laboratory level and preclinical studies.

I did a literature review, and got inspired by David's work. Optical fibres, I discovered, have several advantages over other techniques of radiation detection, being inert and immune to electromagnetic interference. Their tiny dimensions – they were the thickness of my hair, and cut into minute fragments, two to five millimetres in length – their light weight and flexibility, mean they are minimally invasive. This was exciting: these sensors could be used *in vivo*, meaning they could be placed into the accessible tumour itself, or any adjacent tissue requiring monitoring, via the same applicators or needles used for the treatment delivery. I found this truly inspiring, and thought how lucky I was to have landed on my feet with an expert in optical fibre dosimetry as one of my supervisors.

I had the opportunity to evaluate optical fibres for myself when I worked with them for a week or so. It was then that I discovered that they have disadvantages, too. Because they are so small, and transparent, I could hardly see them. I found you had to be very careful when using them not to breathe too heavily, let alone sneeze, for fear of losing them. They were also very expensive.

These practical challenges made me think that, however accurate they might be, they might not be ideal in general application. I started to wonder about other options: whether there might be alternative materials, with similar properties in terms of clinical science, but easier to handle, and mass-produced, hence readily available and affordable.

What was very much on my mind was that I wanted to find a medium that could be utilised in Afghanistan. It was still my plan to return, to work at an advanced level in radiology and radiotherapy. It would be no good for me to find myself in that situation if my expertise lay in techniques that could not be translated to local conditions because they were unsuitable, impractical and costly. In fact, it seemed to me a waste of my time to be working on something that would only ever be of use in wealthy countries. So I gave the matter a lot of thought. To be honest, I couldn't stop thinking about it, and lost so much sleep, lying awake at night trying to think of a solution, that I took to putting my notebook next to the bed, ready to jot down any flashes of inspiration that might arrive in the night.

This undercover activity reminded me of those nights in Iran, when I was studying by lantern-light. But this time, I was trying to be inconspicuous for rather different reasons. It wasn't that I didn't want to be found out, but I was trying not to disturb the sleep of Ibrahim and Zahra, who were in the same room as me, or Sara and the student Sakina, in their bunk beds in the adjacent bedroom.

It was not only those living conditions that were far from ideal. We were struggling with money, which impacted on us all. For example, I couldn't afford the standard school uniform for Zahra, so instead bought a couple of green cardigans from Sainsbury's at a fraction of the cost, and embroidered the school logo onto them by hand. Another time, I was given a hasty introduction to the phenomenon of World Book Day when Zahra brought home a letter from school telling me she should come to school dressed as a character from a book. In Sainsbury's, again, I found that even a cheap costume was around £15, which was half of our weekly grocery budget. So I came home and decided I would have to make a costume myself. In my suitcase I found an embroidered Japanese white top, which I was able to adapt, and in a drawer was some lace from a curtain, which I sewed onto my blue shawl to make a Frozen princess dress. In that outfit Zahra was so happy that she danced all the way to school!

The one-bedroom flat we were living in was owned by the drycleaners on the ground floor, and it occurred to me they might know of any casual work going for Ibrahim, who had been unable to find employment. The proprietor told me that if Ibrahim spent his time distributing publicity leaflets, he would deduct £200 from the rent each month. Ibrahim, being the conscientious man he is, worked very hard for those £200 discounts, which were secured at a pitiful hourly rate of pay.

So Ibrahim started looking at other jobs, and an opportunity came up for him to be a cultural advisor for the UK military. This was working as part of a programme that originated with British forces serving in Helmand province, to build relationships with local community leaders, as a basis for understanding and influencing societies in which the army was operating.

Ibrahim signed up, and was sent to 'ghost' villages within military training grounds, that had been set up to simulate Syrian and Afghan settlements, for troop exercises. The work was intermittent, and for only a few months a year, but whenever Ibrahim was working he would be living away from home and able to return only at weekends, or every other weekend.

This made it more of a challenge for me, having to take the children to separate schools every morning, and collect them in the evenings, when Ibrahim was away and I was working. I was struggling to cope with this, and decided it was something I had to tackle. So I went to Sara's school, and told them that in Afghanistan, right from Year 1, Sara had taken herself to school. I was perfectly confident that such an unusually independent child could manage the same in the UK. Even though, I hastily added, before they could object, I knew that her age did not allow it, but I was happy to absolve the school from that responsibility, and after all, it was only a ten-minute walk… This way, I got a letter of agreement from the school for Sara, which meant I could leave her to her own devices.

Next, Zahra, who was at that time attending a pre-school and after-school club. Once again, I explained my situation, and this time, rather to my amazement, the school agreed to charge me only half-price for her fees.

So now, even when Ibrahim was away, I could go to university during the day, and to the hospital on my work days. What helped even more was that Sakina, the student who was living with us, offered to help me by taking the children to or from the school from time to time.

With all this on my mind, I'm not sure how it was that on one of those sleepless nights I found myself thinking back to my early years in Tehran. Perhaps it was my fixation with our finances, because I remembered that when I was quite young, one of the things I used to do to earn a little money was to buy jewellery glass beads from the market, which could be sewn onto clothing as decoration. Tiny beads, that even as a child I could afford...

Wait a minute! Glass beads – small, mass-produced, resilient, sold at market-stall prices... Could this be what I was looking for? Was it remotely possible that the answer to my search for a suitable dosage detector had been staring me in the face?

There was only one way to find out. The next morning I rushed out and bought what I needed, then headed to the radiation laboratory. I ran tests, checked results, double-checked. Then I took a deep breath. I could hardly believe what I was looking at.

I collected up the printouts and headed to the office of my supervisor, Catharine Clark. We had a general chat about the direction of my PhD, and she asked how I was getting on with using optical fibres.

'OK', I said. 'But I've been wondering. Instead of optical fibres, what if we try using glass jewellery beads?'

She stared at me, then burst out laughing. 'Jewellery beads? Like you sew on your clothes?'

I laughed along with her for a moment. 'Yes! I know! Crazy idea, isn't it?' But then I took the printouts from my bag.

'Actually, I did a trial run in the laboratory just now. I thought you might be interested in the results.'

We had both stopped laughing now. She skim-read the pages, then looked more closely. 'This is amazing. I mean, these results are seriously interesting! Where did all this come from?'

I told her about my 'a-ha!' moment, when the glass beads I remembered from the market, and my search for the ideal detector, came together in a semi-dream, in the middle of the night.

'The more I think about it, Catharine, the more convinced I am that these glass beads could be the perfect medium for a detector. Just think about it. They're inert, not sensitive to humidity, resilient. So they don't have any of the drawbacks of the protein powder detector. They're very cheap and easy to handle, which gives them the edge over optical fibres. They even have holes in the middle, so you can string them into arrays. And of course, they're small enough to go inside patients. They are…'

We almost said it together: 'Exactly what we've been looking for!'

Catharine looked at me. 'This is unbelievable.' She paused. 'Shakar, what if you just focus on jewellery beads for your PhD?'

14

This could change lives

BEFORE I COULD GET to work on my new glass bead project, first I had to persuade my panel of supervisors. This should be a walkover. The project was so obviously bursting with potential, I was sure they would want me to make a start on it as soon as possible. So it was rather disappointing that when I talked through the process, and displayed the results that Catharine had found so amazing, two were all in favour, but the other two not so sure. They each had different reservations, and for a moment I thought I was going to lose the project before it had even started. But once all the objections had been raised, and they started to look at the positives, they concurred that while I couldn't keep everybody happy, it was my project and I had to do whatever I thought best.

This only made me all the more determined.

At that stage I had only run one, simple, uncontrolled lab experiment. The next step would be to complete whole sets of characterisation measurements. Catharine helped me with this by introducing my idea to people at the UK National Physical Laboratory, who were amazed by the results and helped me with a lot of experiments.

It was fascinating to see the international research community springing into action. The NPL dosimetry group took my samples to the Clatterbridge Cancer Centre near Liverpool, and to the carbon ion beam facility of the Heavy Ion Medical Center at Gunma University in Japan. We were told they stood awake and irradiated my samples at four o'clock in the morning, as that was the only slot available on the machine! The Surrey Ion Beam Centre helped by running the compositional analysis of the beads on the back of an ongoing trial for my supervisor, David Bradley, and waiving the fee.

Now we could begin controlled tests that would give us the verifiable results we needed. This meant sounding out hospitals to participate in running trials. In the end, the take-up was much greater than I dared hope: twenty hospitals volunteered to test glass bead radiation detectors. Assuming the results confirmed my predictions, this would give me more than enough data to write up the PhD and finish my thesis.

In approaching the hospitals, I explained how simple glass beads could be used in the complex application of radiotherapy. The beads are positioned at the treatment site, in or on the patient's body. When struck by radiation, the electrons within the atomic structure of the glass are 'excited', and move out of their normal alignment. Quantum physics tells us that this structural change, at atomic level, stores energy. The quantity of that energy is related precisely to the amount of radiation to which the beads have been exposed.

After the patient has been treated, the beads are removed for reading. Fortunately, for my purposes, once the beads have been irradiated, the changes in the atomic structure remain integral for a long period of months, or years. So there is no deterioration during the time it takes in getting the beads from the patient to the reader. Here, they have to be heated to 300 degrees Celsius, at which temperature the excited electrons move back to their original alignment, releasing the stored energy in the form of light.

And this is where the whole process has a diagnostic value: by measuring how much light is emitted, we can calculate faithfully how much energy was stored in the beads, and hence how much radiation was received by the patient at the precise location of each bead. The light emissions are measured with something called a photomultiplier tube – a glass vacuum cylinder capable of extremely sensitive detection of light. The readout from this, after interpretation, gives us the magic figure of the patient's dosage. Glass beads, a heater, a light meter: the system is very simple in terms of materials, but relies on complex quantum physics to make it possible.

I finished gathering all the preliminary characterising data from our radiation lab and the experiments at the Royal Surrey County hospital during the last three months of the first year of my PhD, while the hospital trials were still running, and in my second year, wrote up the report. In September 2013, I submitted my results to the International

Conference on Radiation Dosimetry and Application, held in Prague. It was very well received and I started receiving requests from other research groups, to try my detector in their own labs.

The level of encouragement I got back from those research groups made me start to think seriously about how the glass bead detectors could be commercialised. It felt like a great discovery, but I was concerned that if I did nothing about it, it would remain nothing more than a curiosity. My thesis would sit on a shelf, and nobody else would do anything with the theory. I was the only expert.

Meanwhile, nine months into my first year working on the PhD, I had completed the placement at the Royal Surrey County Hospital. After that I continued to work there as a volunteer trainee medical physicist. Because Ibrahim's earnings were not much, and I didn't have a job, all our savings were used up by then. Once again, I found myself torn between two uncertainties: the unknown potential of my PhD work, and the Cancer Centre job waiting for me in Kabul. Should I stay, or give up and return to Afghanistan?

Ibrahim's own career was also at a crossroads, as the slack periods when he was not required for the military cultural advisor job had given him time to finish the dissertation for his masters in law. The next step was for him to attend his viva voce exam, which could only be done in Kabul. I saw him off at the airport, expecting to pick him up again within a couple of weeks.

While Ibrahim was out of the country, our landlord told me he was giving us notice to quit: he needed our flat for his own staff. In a panic, I got in touch with various letting agents, who all told me the same thing: because I was a student, and didn't have a sustainable income, I would have to give six months' deposit in advance, or failing that, provide a guarantor. We didn't have the sort of money required, and I felt unable to ask anyone I knew to take a gamble and put up the money for us. That ruled out the idea of getting accommodation through an agent.

So I tried a different tack: I went to the Guildford Borough Council offices, explained my situation, and told them that while I knew I was not eligible for any sort of public support, did they have any accommodation I could rent? They told me I had been given a student visa on the basis that I could finance myself during my studies. 'If that is not possible', they began – this is it, I thought, they are going to offer me a lifeline – 'if that is not possible, the only thing we can do is to introduce you to a charity, who could buy you a return ticket to your own country.'

After that, in my spare moments, between looking after the girls and working, I started searching Gumtree for private apartment rentals.

It was not until I had viewed a whole chain of properties that the penny dropped: they don't let studio flats or one-room flats to a family, because it is against the law.

OK, I thought, I don't want to break the law, but at the same time I can't let this defeat me. We need somewhere to live! I would just have to find somewhere anywhere – and use my guile, once again, to forge a way around any legal or contractual mantraps.

The next affordable property that came up on Gumtree was a studio apartment in a modern, low-rise block of flats in a suburb of Guildford. I booked an appointment, and when I went for the viewing, took the children with me. As soon as

Julie, the landlady, saw them she said: 'Oh, I thought it was only you. I didn't realise you had children. I'm sorry, but I can't give it to you.'

I said: 'Look, this is the only thing I can afford. You don't have to worry about the children making a noise. They are not like other children, not brought up running wild. They are basically – how would you say? – bookworms.'

I loved dropping colloquialisms into the conversation, and it wasn't until later that I was told that a stranger might think it odd for me to use this particular expression of my own children. But it was true! Every Saturday I took them to the library, where they borrowed – bookworms! – ten books at a time.

While the landlady was looking my daughters up and down slightly oddly, I sold her my pitch on how her flat could work for us. We were already sharing a one-bed flat with a student, I told her, so this would be a step up. My husband was in Afghanistan 'indefinitely', so he was out of the equation. The bookworms could sleep in a bunk bed over there – I chopped the room into segments with my hands – and I would have a futon rolled against this wall, and that would be enough for us. 'We will be very cosy!' I reassured her.

She told me she would think about it and get back to me. A day later I received an email: she was happy for me to sign the contract. And so we moved into our new home, which had a floor area of precisely ten square metres! It was so small that when somebody was sitting down in the middle, there was no space for anyone else to walk across the room. But at least there was a nice little garden area, where the girls could play outside – I mean, where they could play if there was any time left in the day when they didn't have their heads in their books.

Ibrahim called from Kabul. He had paid all the necessary fees, and had gone to attend his viva exam at the appointed time. But his examiners had not turned up. He made enquiries, and was told that they were not prepared to adjudicate until there were more students ready for the exam. He said: 'Well, you told me to come to Kabul, and I came here, all the way from the UK, which cost me good money and time.' I could tell from his voice that, under that placid, reassured surface, Ibrahim was seething.

He hung about in Kabul for a couple of months, waiting to be called for his viva, but nothing happened. During this time, his health deteriorated – partly, I am sure, because he was becoming distressed about leaving us, and wasting our precious money on this hopeless task. Eventually, with no end to the examiners' standoff in sight, he gave up without taking the viva, and flew back to the UK.

We related this story to Nina and Peter, the couple we had met through Friends International, a few weeks later. They mentioned that they had a friend working for Kentucky Fried Chicken, and knew that there was a vacancy. Would that be of any interest? We were sceptical, because until then every online job application Ibrahim had made had been rejected, and that included a job with KFC. But our friend's friend arranged an interview, and when Ibrahim met the KFC manager in person he was accepted. Life became a bit easier with him having an income.

Zahra had become a close friend of the daughter of another of our Friends International contacts – a Chinese single mum – and used to spend a lot of her spare time at their house. One afternoon I went to pick her up, and while we were waiting at the bus stop, a woman started talking to me. She boarded the same bus as we did, and as I sat down next to Zahra, she said: 'Do you mind if I come and sit beside you? She can sit on the other seat.' She waved Zahra away. This woman asked me a lot of questions, and I felt a bit scared of her. When we got home, I told Ibrahim about the curious incident, and he said I must be careful.

Two months later, at the same bus stop, the same woman got me into conversation, which led to her inviting Ibrahim and me to her house for coffee. 'My name's Angela, by the way,' she mentioned.

I told Ibrahim, who again advised caution, but said: 'I can't see it will do any harm to visit her.' So we went to her house and found her to be the warmest, friendliest person, with nothing more alarming than a natural curiosity about the people around her. We quickly became good friends.

Angela became an invaluable support. For example, when I was too busy I could always ask her to pick up Zahra from school and take her to her home, where I would collect her later. Then, when we moved house from our studio apartment into a one-bedroom flat a mile or so away, Angela was one of a team – our friends Julian, Ian, Nina and Peter from Friends International all joined in – helping to transport loads of our belongings by car.

Angela then looked around the flat. 'Where are you going to dry your clothes?' she demanded. On her next trip, she brought me a couple of airers to use in the garden. As she was leaving she said: 'By the way, over the summer I'm off to Scotland. I'll be staying at my mum's house. Why don't you all come for a holiday?'

So in the summer recess of 2014, we flew EasyJet to

Inverness. Angela's mum lived in a remote farmhouse – this was the first time I heard the word 'croft' – where Angela had grown up. The house had probably not changed much in the fifty years since she had left home. We spent eight days there, and the children loved it. But it made me homesick, being on this farmstead, with the mountains and hills all around, everywhere wildness towering over the timid little patches of cultivation. It was so much like Afghanistan! Except that it was raining most of the time. When there was sunshine, Angela would take us out sightseeing, and in the evening, cousins and sisters would visit and we would sit around chatting.

Once again I felt the sturdiness of the family unit, here as I had known it in Afghanistan. I loved the cosy intimacy of this; the easy conversation; always plenty of laughter. During this time, I became very close to Angela, and found myself sharing concerns and worries with her.

While I was writing up my thesis, I had begun to think about what to do with my discovery of the application of glass beads in radiation dosimetry. I wanted to continue beyond the PhD stage, which meant investigating the market potential and thinking about how to commercialise it. None of that could happen without money, so I also gave some thought to potential sources of funding.

In fact, I had made some tentative enquiries before we left home, and while we were staying at the farmhouse, I received an email: a government funding quango, UK Trade & Investment (UKTI), was opening up a waiting list for applicants, and was I available for an online interview? The bandwidth at the farm wouldn't accommodate Skype, so we drove to Angela's sister's, who lived further down the glen (another new word for me). The interview went well, and I felt optimistic of receiving a grant.

The only difficulty was that the terms of the grant specified a team of at least two people, and I was very much a one-woman band. So, back in Guildford I asked around, and another student agreed to join forces with me. But after a few weeks she flew to the US for a conference, and liked it so much she decided to stay there to complete her post-doctorate. Losing my team-mate meant losing my funding. I frantically started searching for other suitable people, and my friend Roya, who taught Persian at a school in Guildford, told me she knew an architecture student of Iranian origin, Shabnam Jamshidi, who was just graduating from Kingston University, and who might be able to take on the design part of the project. The change was accepted, so to my amazement we secured funding, in the form of a UKTI Sirius Programme Award, of £28,000. This was to fund a study on assessing the market for a radiation detector, and investigating such factors as how best to market it, and what competition to expect.

Suddenly, it was all happening. Sakina, our flatmate, had told me that scholarships were available from something called the Schlumberger Foundation. This is a non-profit organisation supporting education in what are known as STEM subjects: science, technology, engineering and maths. What made it particularly relevant to my case was its Faculty for the Future Fellowships, which are awarded to women who, like me, are from developing and emerging countries, and who want to pursue PhD research in STEM subjects.

That was me exactly! And I was even more impressed when I learned of the programme's long-term goal of promoting gender equality in scientific careers.

I applied for this scholarship in October 2013, when my tuition fee was overdue and I didn't have enough money for rent. There were three stages to the selection process, and it wasn't until April 2014 that I learned my application had been successful, winning me a grant which funded my living expenses and tuition fees for the final year of my PhD.

I also won a Researcher into Innovator award from Surrey University. This gave me a place on a three-month training course, which included three days a month at an intensive 'boot camp'. This gave me some invaluable insight into the realities of commercialisation.

One of the key components of putting my project into the marketplace was the reader used for heating the glass beads and measuring the light they emitted. In the hospital trials, the results had been analysed using what was available – a manual reader. While this would suffice in the laboratory and in trials, it was so time-consuming as to be impractical in a clinical environment. So my immediate task was to design a prototype model for a fully automated reader.

Once this was at prototype stage, the university asked me to enter it into a Santander Universities competition, where I presented the commercialisation under the title True-Invivo. They allocated a mentor, Nigel Biggs, who was entrepreneur-in-residence at Surrey University. Nigel helped me write a proposal, and we got True-Invivo registered as a trading company with Companies House in the last week of 2014. Soon after this, Nigel resigned from his position at the university, and came to work in my company. It made good sense to me for this new post to go to an English-speaking, suit-wearing native, with plenty of experience in business, rather than giving myself the thankless task of having to win acceptance in yet another potentially hostile arena.

At this point I needed to think about the status of my visa. I had arrived in the UK on a student visa, which covered everything I had done up until the foundation of the company. When that happened, I was obliged to switch to a graduate entrepreneur visa (now known as a start-up visa), which entitled me to trade for the first couple of years. But I wanted to look beyond that point, when I knew I would need the greater security of a higher-category visa called an entrepreneur visa (now innovator visa), offering longer-term trading and the bonus of settlement after three years, provided certain conditions were met. The only problem was that, to meet the requirements, I would need a start-up investment of £60,000 in my company. There was no way I could seek financial backers yet, as we had nothing to show: we were still at the ideas stage, without even a patent for the fully automated reader. The only alternative was for Ibrahim and me to save up the money, in the hope of reaching that distant £60,000 target. It looked an impossible task, but we decided to plough on with a kind of blind optimism that perhaps our meagre savings would be bolstered by grants or awards, allowing us to reach the magical sum.

We ended up living a very frugal life. The worst thing was having to say no to the children when they wanted to attend school events that we couldn't afford. Sara's school organised a lot of trips, nationally and internationally, but the typical cost of £1,000 a time was out of our reach. Then there were all the after-school activities, such as music lessons and sports clubs, that we couldn't afford. One of the things that bothers me most now is that it was not just Ibrahim and myself who had to make sacrifices, but we demanded the same of our young daughters too.

Amid all this austerity I experienced moments when doors opened into an entirely different life, tantalisingly close yet out of reach. The one that affected me most was when I was fortunate enough to become sole winner for 2015 of the Massachusetts Institute of Technology's Grant Thornton Entrepreneurial Excellence Award. This dangled in front of me the prospect of being flown out to the States for a two-week placement at some time within the following year that would give me useful advice and insight into how to commercialise my project, and introduce me to prospective investors. In my imagination, I saw it as a fantastic opportunity that would free me, if only for a fortnight, from all those worldly worries.

Meanwhile, though, having committed ourselves, we got on with saving all the money we could from the scholarship and our incomes. We reduced our outgoings as far as we possibly could, broadening our definition of avoidable 'luxuries', shopping carefully in the supermarket for special offers and final reductions, and buying clothes for the children and for ourselves from charity shops. It felt as though that astronomical target of £60,000 would be hanging over us for the rest of our lives.

15

Schrödinger's Equation

In May 2015, I went back to Kabul. The question of what we were doing with our lives, whether we wanted to stay in the UK, how we saw our future panning out, was getting on top of me. I needed to assess the situation in Afghanistan on the ground, to see if there was any realistic prospect in my hopes of returning there to live and work. I had completed writing up my PhD thesis in February, and was waiting for my viva voce, which had been scheduled for 23 June. This seemed the perfect window.

My first priority was to think about what returning to my home country would mean for Sara and Zahra. Their upbringing had been interrupted enough, and the move would depend on sorting out suitable schooling for them. By this time English was their first language, and while we spoke some Farsi at home, they had not picked up enough for regular schoolwork, even though I had been sending them to Persian classes. I discussed the matter with an international school in Kabul, and got their agreement that in the event of our return, I could register the girls at the school.

Next, I needed to sound out the chancellor of the university. I was aware that I had been away in the UK for much longer than originally agreed, and wasn't sure if I would be allowed to pick up from where I had left off. I explained my situation to the chancellor, telling him how much I wanted to complete the re-establishment of the cancer centre, but at the same time was very reluctant to give up my project in the UK. Was there any way I could do both? That would be the most desirable, but least practical, of my various options. To my great relief, and surprise, he told me he would be happy for me to spend six months of the year in Afghanistan, and six months in the UK. He would draft a letter of consent for me to collect later.

Word had got out that I was back in Kabul, and some events were thrown in my honour by faculty scholars. It surprised me that all these people even knew who I was, but my unusual status as an Afghan woman working in the West in medical science research had been picked up by the media, and there had been a couple of pieces on the BBC and Voice of America, as well as interviews with various other TV and radio stations. News of all this had filtered back to Kabul, and these events were to celebrate the achievements in my research.

This gave me the opportunity to talk to a cross-section of Afghan scholars, most – but not all – of whom advised me against returning to Afghanistan. They argued that making the glass bead detectors commercially viable would carry far greater impact than my role in the re-establishment of the cancer centre. 'Look at it this way,' one of them said to me. 'Your colleagues would be more than capable of taking on your responsibilities for the cancer centre, right? But think what would happen if you stop what you are doing in the UK. Your project there will never happen.'

On the other hand, a minority of the scholars advised me not only to carry on with the re-establishment, but to reject the chancellor's proposal outright. They believed my duty was to return to live and work in Afghanistan full-time.

Meanwhile, it was evident that the security situation in Afghanistan was getting worse, particularly since the previous year, when the international army had pulled out. Now, everyone was focused on security, unrest, political and religious turmoil, the threat of an uncertain future. Nobody could look at the bigger picture.

An example of this, from my own area of concern, was when we drafted the radiation legislation for Afghanistan and tried to pass it through our parliament, the National Assembly. This was to permit the IAEA direction of the cancer centre. The bill was rejected, with the giveaway rhetoric: 'We don't need atomic bombs.' I realised then what an uphill struggle it was going to be, to educate them into the application of radiation for medical purposes.

I saw no immediate prospect in Afghanistan and so returned to the UK, without the letter of consent from the chancellor as it was not ready for collection. My mission was only partly accomplished. There might be nothing doing in Afghanistan for the time being, I recognised, but I still did not give up hope that one day it would become possible to resume work on the cancer centre, and I would return. Meanwhile, my entire being remained divided into two: my heart was in Afghanistan, and my head in the UK. When I told Angela, she looked at me very sternly. 'For heaven's sake, Shakar! Why would you even think about going back?' I had learned to respect Angela and take her opinions seriously. But I could not give up the idea of returning home.

Back in Guildford I learned, through one of the Surrey University workshops that I attended, of an alternative to the entrepreneur visa. It was called the exceptional talent visa. When I looked into the provisos, I discovered that this would enable me to continue to work on my project while taking on any other relevant work at the same time. This was a huge advantage over the entrepreneur visa, which allowed only a single line of work. That would have meant that as long as I pursued my project, the only work I would be permitted to undertake at the hospital would have to be voluntary. Since my project was not likely to generate income in the near future, I would soon have a problem, because my Schlumberger scholarship money would be spent, and Ibrahim's earnings would not meet our needs. The exceptional talent visa offered a very significant added bonus: there was no stipulation for funding. I would be able to forget about the uphill struggle to save £60,000.

I approached a firm of solicitors whom the Home Office had indicated would be able to help with my visa application. They told me they would charge £1,200 to explain to me how to apply for the visa. I said, 'No, that's not the kind of help I need. My English is perfectly good enough to read the Home Office website, understand the process and complete most of the application. What I need is someone to help me write the personal statement, because I'm not confident I know how to do it myself.'

I explained all this to Angela, and she suggested that rather than use the solicitors, I could ask her bridge partner Alistair for help. He had a background in government work, and knew all about how to draft a personal statement. So he gave me some instructions, I went home and wrote my personal statement, gave it back to him and he kindly checked and corrected it for me. I put in my application.

I knew that if I got the visa I could take a salaried job, as well as continuing my project. Rather than wait for the visa to come through, I decided to take a gamble and start looking for work right away. This was risky, but as with my flat-hunting, I resolved to go for what I wanted, and tidy up the paperwork later. I came across an advert for a post in the radiotherapy physics department at Queen Alexandra Hospital, Portsmouth. This looked promising, because I knew that Tony Palmer, the head of department, had a good relationship with the head of medical physics at Surrey University, as he himself had been doing his PhD at the same time as me. I applied for the job, and got invited for an interview on 22 June. There was only one snag: the following day, 23 June, was the date of my viva exam.

So I took the draft of my thesis with me when I went for the interview, to read on the Portsmouth train. The train service was particularly bad that day, with cancellations, and it took me three hours to get from Guildford to Portsmouth, when the journey would normally take half that time. Ten minutes before the interview was due to begin I got a phone call, asking if I was coming. 'Yes, I'll be there as quickly as I can!' I explained about the trains. But then there was another spanner in the works, because Google Maps, which I was relying on to get me to the hospital by the quickest route, took me down a dead-end road. I had to walk a huge loop all around the hospital to find the main entrance.

They started asking about when I would graduate from my PhD. 'Well, I have my viva tomorrow. I brought my thesis with me to read on the train on the way down here.'

They asked to see the thesis. They skimmed through, and started asking questions about the ideas and the science behind them. When it came to the clinical questions, the interviewer was speaking so fast, and the sun was shining so brightly on his face that I could not see his lips properly, and I found it almost impossible to understand what he was saying. I asked him to repeat his questions time after time. I lost any confidence that they would hire me, because I was sure they would think my standard of English not good enough.

So I came home feeling quite pessimistic.

In the viva next day, we started with me giving a fifteen-minute presentation of my PhD in front of a panel of all my supervisors, the external examiner and the internal examiner. At the end of my presentation, the external examiner started asking me a question about Schrödinger's Equation. This was a killer question! Schrödinger's Equation is a key result in quantum mechanics, and is a long and complex differential equation governing the wave function of a quantum-mechanical system. 'Would you care to tell the panel how you applied Schrödinger's Equation during your experiments, Ms Jafari?' I replied, quite honestly: 'Off the top of my head, I don't even remember the full details of Schrödinger's Equation!' But I offered to explain how I had applied all the parameters. Then we went through each of the chapters of the thesis, and I answered their questions. The title of the final chapter was Preliminary Investigation of Glass Beads for Hadron Therapy. (Hadron therapy is a type of radiation therapy that uses irradiating beams made of charged particles.) This chapter detailed the pinnacle of my PhD work.

The examiner said: 'Ms Jafari, do you know, the results from this one chapter alone are enough for a full PhD?' I drew a breath, then smiled when he followed it up with a phrase full of old English charm: 'I take off my hat to you.'

They asked me to wait outside in the corridor, while they consulted. It took about half an hour, and when I came back I could see from the looks on their faces that it was going to be good news. 'Congratulations! I'm delighted to say you have passed your viva. And without correction.' The examiner looked at the other members of the panel. 'Well done. I think we would all agree this is a very rare outcome.'

It was such a happy moment, I started to cry. After the congratulations and handshakes, we all went off to have lunch together, as is the custom. Then, just as lunch was drawing to a close, there was a ping on my phone: an email, telling me that I had got the job I had applied for the previous day.

Our whole lives changed. The following week, we all caught the train down to Portsmouth, to check out schools for the girls, and to begin house-hunting. We found a two-bed house in Fratton, a studenty, terrace-house suburb of the city, and before we knew where we were, we had moved to Portsmouth.

I started my new job on 3 August, 2015. Given the options of which shifts to take, I signed up for the late shifts for Mondays and Wednesdays. This gave me Monday and

Wednesday mornings, plus evenings and weekends, for working on the commercialisation of my project.

Earlier in the year, I had won another £50,000 of funding under the Innovation to Commercialisation of University Research, or ICURe programme. Funded by Innovate UK and delivered by SETsquared consortium, this was set up to assist researchers and academics who wanted to begin exploring commercial options for their research. The three-month programme paid me a salary, so I signed a research contract with the university. The grant also provided a pot to cover expenses for specific research into marketing, such as checking out competitors and scouring the field for potential customers. It enabled me to go to conferences, and paid for a visit I made to PTW-Freiburg ('the dosimetry company') in Germany, a leading player in the field of radiation detectors.

On the scientific and technical side I was on my own, as there was no money to hire assistants. But on the business side, we were building up a good team, with Professor Andrew Nisbet and Professor David Bradley both coming in as non-executive directors. Professor Spyrou, unfortunately, had become ill in 2014 and was no longer able to come to the university, but I was able to keep him updated on my project by phone. My previous partner, Shabnam Jamshidi, left to pursue her career in architecture. Nigel Biggs, my CEO, was happy with progress, although I think it worried him that I had taken the risky option of starting my new job in Portsmouth before receiving my exceptional talent visa. But, as I told him at the time, I couldn't keep going without an income. I think he was as relieved as I was when, at the end of August, I received acceptance of my Part 1 Exceptional Talent Visa, meaning that I was back on firm legal ground for working in parallel at the hospital and on my project.

In September, Ibrahim went alone to Afghanistan to visit his family. I asked him if, while he was there, he could go into the office to sign the paperwork on my behalf for the consent letter from the Ministry of Higher Education and from Kabul Medical University. This was the agreement that I could work six months of the year on the re-establishment of the cancer centre. But at the office, Ibrahim was completely taken aback when the piece of paper passed across the counter was not the consent letter, but its total opposite. They gave Ibrahim no option but to sign my resignation letter.

I was really upset about this, because I had been so keen to re-establish the cancer centre, and for all these years one part of me saw it as my absolute goal. But on the other hand, it was a relief. I had been so torn between the two divergent paths in my professional career, and now the choice had been made for me. Or had it? The Afghan mode, I knew, worked in absolutes, and the resignation letter meant I was absolutely out of the running. But as I knew from past experience, much of Afghan bureaucracy is the mess that occurs when two or more absolutes collide. Somewhere, I thought, behind my torn-up contract there would be a file containing the same contract, Sellotaped together. If I wanted to go back, there would be a way.

For now, though, we decided to make the most of our new-found and unexpected sense of liberation. We sold a piece of land we owned in Afghanistan, adding the proceeds to our savings. At the same time, we freed up all the money I was planning to plough into the business for the entrepreneur visa. Suddenly, we had enough for a mortgage deposit.

More house-hunting turned up a three-bedroom semi

that we could afford. Three bedrooms! This was bliss, and wonderful for the children, who were both studying hard and needed space of their own. It was November when we moved in, and I planted the garden with winter flowers, daisies and pansies. Those were the flowers that my father used to plant in our garden.

We had become friends with a relative of my old MSc colleague, Musa, who lived in Portsmouth. He and his wife invited us to spend Christmas at their home, when she was due to give birth, and I was to help her when her baby was born. From this start, we developed a social circle of seven families, all originating from the same province of Afghanistan, and we have met regularly ever since.

The following year, 2016, I flew to Boston, US, with David Bradley for the two-week placement I'd won as part of the Grant Thornton Entrepreneurial Excellence Award. It was a great trip, and I picked up some invaluable tips for commercialisation. But what impressed me more was how everything was so impressive, so grand and affluent. And when I spoke to potential investors, I was in for a real shock. At home we were trying to make our way on stepping-stone grants of a few tens of thousands of pounds each. In the States, they were talking about putting in a 'small investment' of more than a million dollars at a time. It made me wonder not so much whether I should seek American backing, but more whether the project could survive *without* it.

About the same time, I applied for the prestigious Women in Innovation UK Award. This is offered to women whose businesses are not only considered 'innovative', but have ambitions to address some pressing challenge, which might be related to society, the environment, or the economy. Funding comes through the science budget of the Department for Business, Energy and Industrial Strategy, and is awarded by Innovate UK, as part of UK Research and Innovation. The prize is a handsome grant of £50,000, alongside a package of mentoring, coaching and business support. Not surprisingly, it is very competitive.

I was with Nigel the day the results came through, and we were both on the edge of our seats as I scanned the letter. 'Well?' I didn't need to say anything; it must have been written all over my face. 'We won!' It was a win for 'us', of course, the whole team, but I was very aware that it was also a personal award, an award to a woman, and it was truly gratifying for me, both as a woman and as a first-generation immigrant, to get that recognition.

The award was made at a very imposing ceremony in the Houses of Parliament. This was really exciting. I could feel the power coming through the stones of the building, the sense that no authority in the land stood above this, that here you could make anything happen. It made me feel that what I was doing really mattered, was estimable. I don't know if I was reading too much into it, but it felt to me as though, in some way, this ceremony was welcoming and recognising my work on behalf of the nation.

In advance, I had a photo session, and my portrait appeared printed on a huge banner hung in the Palace of Westminster. For some time after, I received phone calls from distant friends and colleagues excitedly telling me that they had seen my face on a banner, as UK Research and Innovation hosted events in various government and university buildings around the UK. There was also a video interview with me talking about what it meant to receive the award, and that was what I saw later at Heathrow Airport.

For the first time, we were able to pay ourselves a small wage from the company, allowing me to reduce my hospital work from five days to four. The bulk of the funds went on hiring a full-time engineer, Mike Stroud, who was an expert in digital imaging. His task was to build the first working prototype of the fully automated reader, which I had designed in my final year of the PhD, and had asked the university to patent. Nigel Biggs persuaded Surrey that most of the work for this had been done in my own time when I was writing up the PhD, rather than during University time. For this reason he was able to secure a better deal with the university, who would normally take 70 per cent from the commercialisation of inventions made under its auspices. In our case, they agreed a levy of just 10 per cent, leaving me the remaining 90 per cent.

With the fully automated prototype built, we managed to secure a first round of investment. This raised our profile, and I received an invitation from Oxford University to be the guest speaker at their Women in Physics conference, for which I had been nominated by the students. I talked a little about my background, by way of introduction, and to my surprise, one of the attendees built on what I said to write a Wikipedia page about me. Around this time, I was also invited to be keynote speaker at the 2018 graduation ceremony of the University of Surrey.

When I took the full-time NHS hospital job, one of my motives was, of course, that I still had it in my mind to go back to Afghanistan to work on the cancer project. To achieve this, I needed to be internationally recognised as an expert Registered Clinical Scientist. This qualification has two routes into it: one gave priority to UK citizens, and so was not for me; the other was awarded in recognition of a work record. I was able to submit a portfolio showing six years' experience in a clinical role, as well as various academic publications. There was a viva exam in York, and in July 2017, I received my qualification as a Registered Clinical Scientist.

Meanwhile I was participating in more and more research work at the hospital. When there was a call for submitting research proposals, I responded by writing up MSc proposals and submitting them to the head of department. Most of these were challenges we had in the hospital that might be solved using the technology my company was working on. This way I ended up supervising a lot of research projects for students from the universities of both Portsmouth and Surrey, which fed into the research side of the company.

But I was worried that I was not able to spend enough family time, especially when the children needed more attention from me as they grew into their teenage years. I had to get a bit of balance into our family life. So we booked a three-week holiday in Afghanistan in August 2018. We stayed with Ibrahim's family in Herat, and with my family, and we met up with plenty of old friends. The highlight was a trip to Bamiyan. This is somewhere I had always wanted to visit: the main — although not very big — city in Hazarajat, in the mountainous centre of the country. An unusual feature is that, because it lies in a confined valley, the airport is right in the centre of the city. Despite that, it is very picturesque, deserving its title of 'Valley of Gods'.

I loved the huge lake, which has I think the biggest natural dam in the world. The colour of the water is such a beautiful blue, and very clear, so you can see everything at the bottom.

One of the main local attractions is the world-famous Buddhas of Bamiyan, carved into cliffs on the edge of the city in the sixth or seventh century CE. The two largest statues were destroyed by the Taliban in 2001, instantly becoming symbols of all that is objectionable about the Taliban: arrogance, destructiveness, intolerance and lack of culture.

We visited Bamiyan as a group, about thirty in total, keeping together because we were afraid of the Taliban, who controlled a lot of the roads. We all travelled in my cousin's minibus, designed to hold just fifteen people, but somehow all thirty of us squeezed in! There is a law against this in Afghanistan, but nobody follows it. We travelled out from Kabul by the safe route, a twelve-hour journey that we knew would avoid any roadblocks. But coming back from Bamiyan, tired and wanting to get home, we took a risk and went on the shorter, four-hour route. When we reached the oasis settlement of Jalriz, lush with its orchards and fields of crops, our worst fears were confirmed when we found the Taliban in control, a militia thronging the road. They stopped our minibus and prowled around it, with their black clothing and long beards and guns. We were very scared of them, but luckily for us they just asked for some transit money, which my cousin gave them, and they sent us on our way.

Despite the Taliban, it was a wonderful trip, and set me thinking once again about the possibility of returning to pursue my career where, I felt, it might do the most good. My head was swimming with such ideas when we got home to the UK. I went and took a shower, and it was while I was washing that I found the lump in my breast. 'What's this?' I asked Ibrahim. We decided I should call the GP.

16

I thought it was a joke

THAT WAS ON THE MONDAY. I went to the local medical practice early the next day, where the GP reassured me there was nothing to worry about.

'There's a 98% chance of it being a benign cyst,' she said, which sounded like a very good prognosis. 'But it's as well to get it checked.'

She referred me to a breast-screening clinic at the hospital for a mammogram, a fortnight later, on 26 September. It couldn't be anything too serious, I thought, if it could wait two weeks. But after I had had the mammogram, I was called back into the surgery to discuss the results. As I was sitting down, I noticed the monitor on the side of the desk, where the consultant had put up a display of my mammograph. I had seen so many of these in my working life that I knew what tell-tale signs to look for. In a glance, my eye was drawn to one corner of the display, where there was a focused white patch. Sometimes it is bad to know too much… I didn't have to be told what it was. I was looking at an enlarged lymph node, and knew beyond doubt that I had breast cancer.

I was totally unprepared, and the shock hit me almost like a physical blow, making me stagger sideways as I sat down. The GP had thought it was a benign cyst, and I had…what? Agreed with the GP, or believed her without knowing, or simply wanted to believe? I don't think I had been trying to fool myself, but on the other hand, why had my brain, usually so enquiring – so diagnostic – kept so quiet? I couldn't work out how my mind had, like my body, been thrown so much off balance. Mentally I was not the least prepared for cancer, and all of my professional experience and knowledge did nothing to make it any easier. I felt so entirely afraid. I was silently crying, and in shock.

After this, everything happened quite quickly. All of it felt strangely out of my control, as though I was no longer a sentient being but a kind of specimen in a laboratory. After the mammogram they conducted sonography, also called ultrasound. They rubbed gel onto the surface of my body and then took readings using a probe pressed against the skin. This works rather like radar, firing high-frequency sound waves into the body, and measuring their echo as they reflect back from the various internal structures. The data is a live video feed, an easy-to read moving image that contributes to an accurate diagnosis.

The sonograph located a tumour in my breast about the size of a boiled sweet. To find out more about the tumour itself, they gave me a biopsy. This felt very much like the bad cop to the good cop of the sonograph: painful and intrusive, and relying on old-fashioned brute force. The procedure I had is called core needle biopsy, where an inserted hollow needle, attached to a spring-loaded tool, snips 'cores' of breast tissue from the suspicious area. It's hard not to shout 'Ouch!' on each snip. Several snips are necessary.

When all the results were gathered in, I found myself sitting in a small room with the surgeon. *My* surgeon. He said that from the evidence of the tumour and the spread to the lymph nodes, it was clearly a malignant cancer. He was thinking the process of treatment would be chemotherapy first, then surgery, then radiotherapy, following up with antibody drugs and hormone therapy later on, depending on the spread of the cancer. The first step would be further diagnostics: a CT scan and an MRI scan.

When we went through the questionnaire prior to booking the scans, the last question was 'Are you pregnant?'

'No, I don't think so, but hang on a minute, I'm a couple of days late with my period.'

'OK. In that case you need to do a test.'

I came home and the next day did a pregnancy test while Ibrahim was at work. I couldn't believe the result: it was positive. I rang the GP and told her, but said that I suspected it might be a false positive because of my hormone imbalance, due to the cancer. We had been trying for another baby for a year or so, but I thought my age — I was 41 — meant that it might no longer be possible. However unlikely it might seem, the GP reminded me, we need to know for certain. She booked a blood test, for me to take a couple of days later.

Meanwhile I had an interview, in response to a grant application, with Innovate UK in London the next day.

I travelled up on the train with Nigel, the CEO of the company, and when we were walking over Waterloo Bridge I told him about the positive results, quipping that this was only happening to add another layer of complexity to our lives. I couldn't get it out of my mind, and during the interview found myself dwelling on my situation, of having just been diagnosed with cancer, and now testing positive for pregnancy. In some twisted way, I thought it was a joke. Suddenly, I found myself laughing out loud.

The next day, I took the blood test. Positive! I panicked, rang my GP, and explained about the result. 'So, what do you want to do?' she asked me quietly. I knew exactly what she meant. I told her that I couldn't see how the baby would be able to survive chemotherapy, so the best thing would be for me to have a termination, as soon as possible. There was a pause, then the GP said: 'Phone this number and make an appointment. Tell them I've referred you.'

I phoned to arrange the termination, and was given an appointment in ten days. During that period of waiting for the termination, and to see the GP again, I realised the lump was growing faster than you would expect. So I rang the hospital, and they booked me an appointment with another surgeon, Dr Masooma Zaidi, who was able to see me at short notice.

I talked her through my medical complications, to explain why I needed a termination. She took it all in, then a thought struck her. 'Can you just explain again? Is this an unwanted pregnancy?'

'No,' I said. 'We have been trying, but I thought I was too old.'

'Why, in that case, do you want a termination?'

For the obvious reason, I explained: it's not possible to save the pregnancy through the cancer treatment.

Dr Zaidi's reply took me completely by surprise: 'Look,' she said. 'It is possible. We can change your treatment plan. If you really want this baby, please – *please* – reconsider your decision.'

I told her what Ibrahim had said to me, a couple of nights earlier – that the priority was my health, and I should do whatever it takes to get through the cancer treatment. So keeping the pregnancy would only be an option, I explained, if there was no adverse effect on me.

She said: 'No, there won't be much adverse effect, but we will need to see the pathology results to assess the tumour's dependency on the hormones. This is because some of the treatments are not compatible with pregnancy.'

I came home, talked to Ibrahim, and he said we must tell the children. So, over dinner I told them what was happening, with the cancer and with the pregnancy, the termination I had booked and the possibility of keeping the baby. I put it to the girls: 'Look, let's think about the worst scenario. If I don't survive the treatment, you might end up with a new baby and no mum. So what do you think I should do? Should I proceed with the termination?'

My daughter Sara, who was then seventeen, said something amazing: 'Look, Mum, Zahra and I are old enough to help Dad if, God forbid, only the baby survives. So don't worry about that. And of course, we'd love you to have the baby. But for all of us, the most important thing will always be your own safety and your health.'

For now then, we agree that I would keep the baby, and change the treatment plan. But if at any stage the pregnancy appeared to be having a negative impact on the treatment, we would abort.

When the biopsy results came back, the results showed that the tumour was very aggressive. The surgeon spelled it out: 'You're not going to have a lumpectomy; we need to completely remove the breast and also the lymph nodes. This won't affect your decision over the pregnancy, because the type of treatment is the same – it's just the extent of the surgery that has changed. On the plus side, it does mean that you no longer need the CT or MRI scans, because we are going for radical surgery.' I knew that this was good news for the baby, because those scans are not good for pregnancies.

I was given a date for surgery, but because the tumour was growing so quickly they also put me at the head of the waiting list, so that if there were any cancellations I could be treated sooner. As it happened, there was a cancellation, and I received a call to say they could bring the surgery forward by one week.

We were, of course, delighted by the news. But when Ibrahim told his manager at KFC, where he was then working, that I was having surgery the following week, on the Monday, so he would like to take the day off, the reaction was not so enthusiastic. The manager said very bluntly that she was not interested in listening to his story, and refused him a day's leave.

Ibrahim was very upset, and told me he could not face going to work any more. So he handed in his notice. It was grossly unfair, because he was a good worker who had never taken liberties.

I hardly had time to assimilate this bad news before going to hospital on the Monday where I underwent surgery.

There were no complications, and I was soon sent home to recuperate. To monitor the baby closely, the hospital put together an interdisciplinary team to cover and consult on both the pregnancy side and the cancer side. I also had regular check-ups with Nicole Bailey, my midwife. By the time I had recovered from the surgery I was at the twelve-week stage in the pregnancy, and was told it was now safe for me to proceed with chemotherapy.

Everything appeared to be going according to plan, but during this time I was very anxious. Since the start of my treatment there had been a lot of emotional turbulence. I realise now that Ibrahim and I had been both completely shocked and partly in denial. Each time we got a pathology result, we would tell each other that whatever they had found might be an anomaly, which would be negated by the next result. I genuinely believed that the pathology report post-surgery would find that all these things were just a mistake, and everything was normal. Of course, when I saw the results it was very difficult for me to admit the reality. Another stumbling block was that I found it hard to accept the limits on my abilities: it was very frustrating having such a lot of work to do, and not being able to do much of it.

In such strange circumstances I was beginning to feel isolated. I called in at the Macmillan cancer charity office in the oncology ward at the hospital, where the staff were wonderfully warm and understanding. They came to the rescue, putting me in touch with an organisation called Mummy's Star, which supports women having cancer treatment during or in the year after pregnancy, as well as their families. I went onto their forum and saw pictures of mums and their toddlers who had been through all of

SHAKAR: A WOMAN'S JOURNEY FROM AFGHANISTAN

that, looking so normal and happy. It was a tremendous reassurance. I became a regular in the Macmillan centre, talking through difficulties, picking up tips and signing up for various programmes, including hypnotherapy.

I did a lot of research, reading articles on the physical and mental development of children whose mothers had undergone chemotherapy during pregnancy. This taught me that there was about a five per cent chance that the baby would be born with physical abnormalities or a mental condition. That might have sounded alarming, but I took strength from it, turning the statistic on its head: there was a ninety-five per cent chance that we would have a completely normal baby.

Since Ibrahim and the girls had arrived in the UK, we had become even closer to my friends Paul and Fran, and had been invited to their house for almost every Sunday lunch. They were so close that we thought of them as our English parents. And now they did something extraordinary: when I was diagnosed with cancer, although they were about to sell their house and move to Yorkshire, Paul and Fran took the house off the market. 'We can't leave while you're still going through treatment,' they told us. 'The move can wait.' They visited us regularly and offered much-needed support.

Chemotherapy started on 3 December 2018. Not long into my sessions I found I was physically very fatigued, and decided to take sick leave from the hospital. Most of the time I spent lying down, from the combined effects of the chemotherapy and pregnancy. But there was still a lot of work that needed doing in the company. We had won the medical catalyst award that we applied for with Innovate UK. Then there was the commercialisation work, that I felt I had to do myself, that nobody else knew how to do. We held weekly team meetings at my house, when I was able to sit for one hour, or at the most, two hours. Then I would wind the meeting up, feeling drained and faint, and when everyone had gone I'd go back to bed and rest. I even managed to attend one of the patent interviews online when I was lying down in a dark room, using audio but with the webcam disabled, so that they could not see me. It was both tiring and stressful.

I went back to the Macmillan Centre. One of their counsellors talked me through my problems and gave me some useful tips on how to manage expectations when I was unable to function at full capacity. 'How will people know they shouldn't expect prompt replies to their emails unless you tell them? It might take the pressure off if you post an auto reply explaining that you are undergoing cancer treatment and unable to answer emails.' That sounds like such a small thing, but my previous sense of denial meant I had been unable to tell people, which had made matters worse because I felt obliged to carry on in the usual way, when I didn't have the energy to do so.

I kept my hair by wearing a cold cap. This is like a high-tech bathing cap, which freezes your scalp during treatment, so that when the chemotherapy drugs are at their highest concentration in your blood, they don't pass through the frozen vessels, and the hair is little affected. The cold cap I had was actually slightly small for me and didn't cover all my scalp, so I lost some hair behind my ears and at the top of my neck. I don't know why keeping my hair mattered so much, but for some reason – perhaps because it would make me feel better to look more normal – it was very important for me. I was pleased I never had to wear the wig they gave me.

A turning point was the three-month scan of the baby. For the first time, I saw arms, and legs, and head, all complete. A real, living baby – my baby! It made me pick up hope. Until then I had not dared to buy much baby stuff because there had been so much uncertainty; still a chance of abnormality, of termination, of still birth. But on the wave of those scan results, I bought some knitted dresses they were selling for charity in the maternity department. After this, I made it a ritual: each time I had an appointment or a scan, I would buy some new item of clothing for the baby.

At home I would give myself baby time, when I would look at those dresses, and touch the swell of the unborn baby. It dawned on me, slowly but with increasing conviction, that if it had not been for the pregnancy, my situation could be much worse. The hormone changes brought about by the pregnancy had pushed the tumour towards the surface, towards discovery. Without the baby, I might not have been diagnosed until a much later stage. And now, I had to do all I could to help him or her survive, because I felt that he or she had already saved my life.

Meanwhile, Ibrahim needed to earn a wage, because I would only receive three months sick leave on full salary, with another three months on half pay, and after that, nothing. The only source of income at that point would be Ibrahim's work, and of course he was now unemployed. But he had learned to drive while we were in Guildford: my friend Roya, the Persian teacher, had given him her old car that was due to be scrapped but still had a few months' MOT, and she took him out for driving lessons. Our friend Angela had also stepped in, with driving lessons in her car. So now we agreed that his best course of action would be to apply to Portsmouth City Council for a private hire driver's licence, which would open up a whole range of alternative jobs.

Ibrahim quickly went on to successfully pass both written and practical driving tests. By November, when I was three months pregnant, he had rented a car, but that turned out to be a source of further stress. It was an old car, and each time he drove it there was a new problem, with the lights or the battery or some other essential function going on the blink. And then, when the car was parked in front of the house, somebody collided with it, and drove off without stopping. The damage was not severe – just some dents on the bumpers – but it felt like the last straw.

I told Ibrahim that we were already under so much stress that we might as well just buy a car. So in December we bought a hybrid Toyota Auris on finance, and he got work as an Uber driver. One great advantage of this was that, because the hours were so flexible, he was able to take me to the hospital and bring me home. He was his own boss, and didn't have to ask permission of a manager.

There was a scan at the five months mark in mid-February, showing all the internal organs, and telling us that it was a boy. To our relief, all the indications were that the baby was healthy and developing well.

But the following month, at the 30-week stage, I had another scan which showed the baby appeared not to be developing any further, or gaining weight the way he should. Despite Sara feeding me smoothies using all sorts of nuts and nutritious ingredients to help make the baby grow, it looked as though he had made his mind up that the pregnancy had gone on for long enough. The doctors planned an induction, and in the meantime, put me on a schedule of scans every two weeks.

This 30-week scan also coincided roughly with my last session of chemotherapy, on 20 March. With a great feeling of release at the end of the chemo, I was able to turn my mind towards work, which had not been receiving as much attention as I would have liked. At the top of my list was the forthcoming European Society of Radiotherapy and Oncology (ESTRO) annual conference, which I very much wanted to attend, to showcase my project, and exhibit our automatic reader and associated technology. The only problem was, it was being held in Milan.

It was a great risk, I knew, because someone who had been undergoing chemotherapy was quite likely to give birth early, due to the combined effects of mental stress, hormone imbalances in the body, and stress from the toxic chemotherapy drugs. But despite all the advice not to travel in my condition – or perhaps I should say 'conditions', plural – I persuaded my doctor to write a certificate of my fitness to attend the conference.

In the last week of April, Ibrahim and I flew to Italy with Nigel and Mike, our company's engineer, all of us quite fearful about the pregnancy. But we had nothing to worry about: the conference was a success; the baby did not arrive early; and when we flew back, I was still pregnant, still viable.

It was in the airport terminal, at passport control, in the slowest of all queues, that we noticed they were screening footage of occasions such as the previous year's wedding of Prince Harry and Meghan Markle, and the London Olympic Games…events, I suppose, that showcased a proud, ceremonial UK. And in among them was my own video, in which I was talking about receiving the Women in Innovation Award, waving the flag for the UK as an attractive and hospitable environment for start-up opportunities – the video, that is, of the old me, or to be more accurate, the recent me, the untrammelled scientist and entrepreneur, in control of her own destiny, looking down on this latest incarnation, seven months pregnant, undergoing treatment for breast cancer, exhausted and shell-shocked. I felt almost like raising one weary hand to wave at that distant other self.

The baby was induced about two weeks later, on 18 May 2019, at 37 weeks. We named him Sina. He was absolutely perfect, and we were overjoyed.

17

Conclusion

THERE WAS NEVER MUCH doubt that the Taliban would take back control of Afghanistan when America and its allies withdrew. They had been building strength for years, as we saw for ourselves at the roadblock at Jalriz during our visit in August 2018. By the time a peace treaty was signed between the US and the Taliban in 2020, the country's fate was virtually sealed.

But when it happened, it was heart-breaking to see how quickly Afghanistan fell. In August 2021, as the remaining foreign military forces pulled out, the country's weakened administration was left powerless against the Islamic fundamentalists. A lightning ten-day sweep across the country saw a string of cities fall to the Taliban, culminating in their capture of the capital, Kabul, on 15 August.

President Ashraf Ghani fled to Abu Dhabi, admitting: 'the Taliban have won.'

The insurgents carefully managed the shocking images of panic and chaos that were screened across the world, as thousands of terrified civilians rushed to Kabul airport in a frenzied scramble to board the last flights out of the country. None of us will ever forget the scene of those poor young people trying to balance on the nacelle of a transport plane, and the pilot just taking off, so that they fell off and died. By 30 August, it was all over, and the Taliban celebrated the departure of the last American and allied forces.

Since then, the plight of Afghans has steadily worsened. Elements of the already frail social and economic infrastructure are either being dismantled or left to collapse, with two-thirds of the population needing humanitarian assistance, malnutrition rates increasing, the healthcare system crumbling, mass unemployment and poverty, a collapse of the housing market, and the kind of figures for migration and displacement we usually associate with natural disasters. There has been a significant rise in attacks targeting Shia, Hazara and other minorities.

In the circumstances, it is no wonder that all of my own family either left the country in anticipation of Taliban rule, or fled as a consequence of it. We are now widely dispersed.

My eldest brother, Mohammad Baqer, became a professional tailor, working for many years in Iran and Turkey. He now lives in Barcelona with his wife and eight-year-old daughter, and runs a Mexican restaurant with his friends.

Masumeh took a degree in psychology, and taught at a primary school in Afghanistan until the Taliban took control of the country in 2021. She and her husband, who was a telecommunications engineer in Kabul, fled to Pakistan with their two sons. The following year they received a humanitarian visa from Brazil, and now teach in a refugee and migrant camp in São Paulo.

Hakima was the artistic member of the family, focusing on art and graphics at high school. Her husband worked as an interpreter for the Canadian armed forces. She was in her final year at Kabul University, studying Arabic languages, when they were granted protection by the Canadian government. They emigrated to Ottawa when she was pregnant with their first child, and now have two sons, aged nine and seven.

Ali Reza studied electronic engineering, and worked for an American mine disposal company in Herat. After one of his colleagues was killed in 2014, he moved to America with his wife and baby daughter. As well as the girl, now aged nine, they have a four-year-old boy, and live in Texas, where Ali Reza works for a car-repair company.

As for my mum, to my heartfelt relief she is no longer in Afghanistan, but is living happily in another part of the world with my younger brother, his wife and their new-born baby.

We have other friends and colleagues who have also chosen to emigrate, and my thoughts return in particular to some friends who fled Afghanistan and went to Ukraine, where they are currently living in Kyiv.

I'm very aware that I have been fortunate in many ways. I have had the wonderful support of Ibrahim, whom I have to thank for his kindness, tolerance and good humour. He has done what very many Afghan men would not have done, in sacrificing a career of his own to endlessly support me and enable our family unit to survive. I'm so grateful that our children have turned out so well, my bookworm daughters flourishing academically and our son a constant delight.

The timing of our migration to Iran was fortuitous too, as, had we arrived in the country only a year or so later, I would have been prohibited from some of my education opportunities. I'm very conscious that the situation in Iran, particularly in respect of women, has become much more precarious since the time my family lived there.

I'm also lucky to have arrived in the UK when I did. Policy towards immigrants and international students is in a state of flux, and it is not clear that the current administration would have allowed me the same latitude in pursuing my education, having my family join me, or founding my business in this country, under present or proposed legislation. As I write this, for example, the UK government has recently tightened the immigration rules to limit the number of dependents international students can bring to the UK. The home secretary has hit out at international students, whom she accuses of abusing the student route as a means to bring relatives to the UK. So it might have been that, rather than Ibrahim and the girls coming to me, I would have had no option but to return to the uncertainties of Afghanistan.

An insight into the status of Afghans in the West came to me in a slightly roundabout way. My daughters were offered roles in a film called *Bachaposh*, directed by Katia Scarton-Kim and shot in Calais, about the migrants and the refugee camps. Sara played the lead character, Nadim, and Zahra took the role of one of her sisters. I went out with them, and on the last day I was sitting in the car with the producer, at about three in the morning, waiting for the call telling us they had a 'wrap', the completion of shooting. We got the call, but it was not what we were expecting. The film crew, about twenty in all, had unknowingly strayed into an unauthorised zone, when the police arrived. They spotted Sara, who had been made up with blood and bruising, and started to question her.

'What are you doing?'

'Playing in a movie.'

'Where is your passport?'

'I don't have it.' (It was in our hotel room).

'Where are you from?'

'Afghanistan.'

At this point the entire crew was arrested. They were taken to the police station, which is where they were calling us from. At the police station I was asked for my passport and visa, which, like Sara's, were in our hotel in Dunkerque, a ninety-minute round trip away. Somehow I was able to persuade the gendarmerie to check out my credentials on Google and Facebook, and – implausible though it may sound – to accept this as proof of our identities. Everyone was released, and on the way out an officer told me I was very fortunate to be so famous! Yes, I thought, very fortunate; and how different from the fate of most other Afghans who find themselves in Calais.

In September 2021, all of our family applied for British citizenship, which I suppose marked the point when we realised we were unlikely ever to be able to return to Afghanistan to live. There were stringent hurdles to pass through, such as proving our knowledge of English, passing the 'Life in the UK' test, and – fingers crossed – being of good character. Having met the targets, we attended a citizenship ceremony and emerged as fully fledged British citizens. All I remember of the ceremony was Sina trying to climb the windows, and having to be taken out screaming! Afterwards, Ibrahim told me he felt as though he'd reached the top of a mountain: 'knackered and elated, all at once'.

To bring the story of my project up to date: eight hospitals are currently involved in testing our glass bead detectors, on top of the twenty previously involved in the initial audit. Royal Marsden, for example, is using beads for an audit of brain radiosurgery. An interesting case is Bristol Hospital, where they use beads for measuring the output of the Gamma knife radiotherapy machine, most often used to treat brain tumours. The machine transmits such a narrow field of radiation that actual measurement was previously not possible, and instead, ball-park figures were obtained using Monte Carlo calculations, which rely on repeated random samplings to obtain numerical results. Now the beads are providing empirical data.

Like so many businesses, we were hit by the Covid pandemic, which slowed development and made it harder to seek investment. We are currently getting back on track, with fresh plans to unveil the beads detectors at two American conferences. This is potentially a big deal for us, as I was very impressed with the funding and support on show when I visited the States in 2016 for the MIT Grant Thornton Entrepreneurial Excellence Award, and it struck me at the time that this would be a very good place for us to expand our business. In 2023, at Nigel Biggs' suggestion, I moved into the role of CEO of the company, with Nigel himself taking on the responsibilities of chief operating officer.

Having established myself in the UK, one of the people I particularly wanted to reconnect with was Mrs Nasrin Bastani, the headteacher who had been so supportive in persuading my dad to let me continue my high-school education. After we left Iran, I made many attempts to track her down using Google, Facebook and so on, with no success. But one day in my final PhD year, when I was in the lab, I tried Facebook again and found her name. The profile picture bore some resemblance, but I thought it might not be her, as this was a much younger person. I posted a message, saying something like: 'I am searching for my teacher, who I want to thank because her action completely changed the direction of my life. I am not sure if this is you, because your picture does not look right.' I received a reply a few days later: 'Yes, I do remember you, Shakar Jafari, and I am glad to hear from you after all this time. The picture is of me, but it's an old one, because that is the way I want to look.' I told her what I was doing, and thanked her, and in her reply she said my message had made her cry, because as a teacher she had no way of knowing the long-term consequences of her good or bad actions, and she was so glad to find that I was in a happy situation.

So we became friends again, and she later offered to assist if I wanted to write my life story. She suggested she could help me get it published in Persian. I made a start, and got as far as writing up my high-school days, the time when my Persian literature teacher, Mrs Maliha Shakoori, gave me a notebook and a poem of divination. Remembering this made me wish I could find her too, and thank her for her support. When I mentioned this to Mrs Bastani, she called on her friends in the Ministry of Education to check the database of teachers, where they found Mrs Shakoori's number. We were put in touch, eliciting another moment of great joy for me.

Somehow these renewed contacts made me feel as though that particular attempt to write my story had already achieved its purpose, and I did not pursue compiling it beyond my mid high-school years. I still wanted to have the story written, but realised at this stage that the book would need to be published in English, and my idea of writing it in Persian and having it translated was impractical. So I enlisted the help of a writer, John Bevis, who is a friend of my friend Angela.

Apart from all else, this has been a spiritual journey for me. Like my father, and his father before him, I have tried to keep an open mind and show respect towards other religions. When I was at high school, I read lots of philosophical and religious books, but found none of them more convincing than the physics lesson when I learned about Einstein's equation of matter and energy ($E=mc^2$), as a way of understanding how the universe, and matter itself, can be formed out of energy.

I kept studying other religions, including Japanese and Indian, and when I came to the UK, I met Julia, who was running Bible study sessions, through Friends international. Julia's classes helped me not only with understanding the Bible and Christianity, but also in practising my spoken English during discussions with Julia and two other friends in particular, Hugh and Rebecca.

While still trying to understand the depth and context of each religion, one night I dreamed of my father. I asked him how the eternal world feels. He smiled and said nothing. When I asked him if could show me Imam Mahdi, the saviour, he looked into my eyes and then turned around. I thought he was going to lead me to the Imam, but he just made a 360-degree turn and looked back into my eyes. I said: 'But this is you! I asked for Imam Mahdi!'

He replied: 'Yes, the truth is this. You yourself need to be Imam Mahdi.'

I was shocked, and woke up confused and shaking from what I had seen in my dream. I felt the pillars of my belief had been shaken. Since then, I have felt much more tolerant of people with different religious backgrounds. No religion seems superior to any other to me. What matters about having religion – or not having it – is how it helps the person to live a happy and purposeful life. Resolving this has made me feel I have reached the inner peace that I was after.

One of the reasons I wanted to write this book is my increasing concern at the effects of the Taliban junta on the women of my country. The treaty drawn up by the West, led by the United States, incorporated a threat of reduced financial support that it was hoped would influence the Taliban's behaviour, in particular towards the protection of women's rights. That incitement was simply ignored. It flies in the face of the Taliban's austere vision of Islam, upheld by their supreme leader, Hibatullah Akhundzada and his consortium of Afghan clerics, which opposes education, particularly for women and girls.

Women have seen their rights obliterated, starting with the dissolution of the Ministry of Women's Affairs. Women and girls have been ordered to be escorted by a male relative whenever appearing in public, where they must wear the hijab and cover their faces. The religious police have said they would prefer it if women simply stayed at home, full stop. Women have been banned from making long-distance journeys alone, and prohibited from going to parks, funfairs, gyms and public baths. Most disturbingly, at the time of writing, all local and foreign non-governmental organisations (NGOs) have been told to stop female employees from coming to work. This will have a widespread devasting effect, as it denies essential, life-saving services to women and children, and removes the only source of income for thousands of Afghan families. These laws are strictly enforced by the notorious Ministry for the Promotion of Virtue and the Prevention of Vice.

Education for women and girls has been particularly hard hit. In March 2022, the Taliban authorities blocked teenage girls from attending secondary school, just one week after the Ministry of Education announced that schools would open for all students. Soon after the Taliban takeover, universities were forced to implement new rules, including gender-segregated classrooms and entrances, and women were only permitted to be taught by female professors or old men. A year into power, and less than three months after thousands of girls and women sat university entrance exams across the country, the Taliban announced there was to be an indefinite wholesale ban on university education for all the country's women.

Wanting to do what I could to help this situation, in September 2021, I became chairperson and programme coordinator of the Education Bridge for Afghanistan (EBA). This is a non-profit organisation established by a group of volunteer education activists, members of the Afghan diaspora, international philanthropists and women's rights activists. Our aim is to provide free access to an online education platform for secondary-level girl students in Afghanistan. We campaign for equal learning opportunities for Afghans, irrespective of where they live, and offer a platform for Afghan students to link with international opportunities, knowledge resources and further education. As well as secondary-level education, online services include personal development counselling, vocational training, teacher training and language courses.

One purpose of this book is to raise awareness of the plight of Afghan women and girls, and to spread the word of organisations such as EBA that are trying to help. It is my hope that this, the story of one Afghan woman, will add one more voice to the chorus of international opposition to their oppression. I would love to think that, somehow, my story might give hope to a disadvantaged girl in my country, struggling as I did. That is the message I would like to end with: encouragement to all those, women especially, working or thinking of working in the fields of education and health who have been touched by my career; and an expression of my belief that we all – again, women especially – have the ability to improve our lives and the lives of those around us by the power of belief, conviction and ethics, by our knowledge and our education.

Acknowledgements

I WOULD LIKE TO EXPRESS my gratitude and thanks to:

My headteacher, Mrs Nasrin Bastani, who convinced my father to let me go to high school; and my teacher, Mrs Maliha Shakoori, for supporting me and giving me hope during my darkest days at high school.

Mr Salehi, and Halima Jan, his wife, for their support and help with my marriage.

UNHCR for the DAFI (Albert Einstein German Academic Refugee Initiative) scholarship I received during my undergraduate studies, without which it would have been almost impossible for me to continue my university studies.

The chancellor of Kabul Medical University and the Ministry of Higher Education in Afghanistan between the years 2004 and 2015 for trusting my ability to lead the cancer centre re-establishment project, and who supported my further studies.

My special thanks go to the International Atomic Energy Agency (IAEA) for sponsoring my MSc and clinical placement; the University of Surrey for the Overseas Research Scholarship that enabled me complete my PhD, and for their support in patent applications and with the commercialisation of my research outcomes.

My heartiest gratitude goes towards the supervisors of my Msc, my PhD and the commercialisation of my project: Professor Nicholas Spyrou, who taught me how to make research impactful and how to come up with innovative ideas; Professors David Bradley and Andrew Nisbet and Dr Catharine Clark, who opened my eyes on how to perform high- quality research, and who have continually supported me in my journey towards commercialisation; Dr Walter Gilboy, who helped me understand the fundamentals of thermoluminescent dosimetry at the beginning of my research.

I would like to thank the Schlumberger Foundation for awarding me the Faculty for the Future Scholarship at the critical point when I was about to give up my PhD studies due to financial difficulties.

Nigel Biggs, my business mentor, past CEO and current COO of the TrueInvivo company I founded, who taught me the reality of life in the business world and the alphabet of business. All the advisors (George Sutherland, our chairman; Simon Devonshire, our business advisor; Dr Alexandra Stewart and Dr Catharine Clark, our medical advisors) and our non-exec directors: Professors David Bradley and Andrew Nisbet, engineer Mike Stroud and Chris Budley) and investors in TrueInvivo, who put their trust and money into our team and my ideas; and Innovate UK KTN, UK Trade & Investment (now Department for International Trade), and SETSquared for the awards and support given to my business.

Many thanks to Dr Tony Palmer, the head of the medical physics department, Mr John Kearton, my line manager, and Dr David Nash, my work supervisor, and the rest of my colleagues for supporting my research ideas during my work at the radiotherapy department of the Queen Alexandra Hospital, Portsmouth. Thanks also to the hospital's radiotherapy physics department for not only helping with my radiation treatment, but also for supporting me as colleagues after my return to work, and to the management team for adjusting my workload as advised by occupational health.

I would like to thank the oncology team for enabling me to receive cancer treatment while keeping my baby. In particular Dr Masooma Zaidi, who first thought of changing my treatment to make this possible, and my midwife, Nicole Bailey, who looked after me during my pregnancy.

Thanks to Friends International Guildford for helping and supporting me and my family with settling in a new country and understanding its culture. It meant a lot to be surrounded by people whom I could trust when I had just arrived in the UK, where I had no friends or relatives, and I am so glad to have made such lifelong friends as Nina and Peter, Ruth, Julia, Ian, Julian, Eddy, Hugh and Rebecca, Roselyn, Saffron and Matthew, and Cherry.

Special thanks go to Paul and Fran, our British 'parents' who supported us during all the ups and downs of our life in the UK; to Angela, who has been such a sincere friend to me and my family, and Angela's children Alison and John; also to Alistair David Pearson, who helped me with my special talent visa application.

I would like to thank our friend John Bevis for being such a great ghostwriter; and everyone at Eye Books, in particular publisher Dan Hiscocks and my editor, Simon Edge, who helped me achieve my dream of publishing my life story.

I am very grateful to Dr Batool Haidari and Mr Assadullah Shafai, who read my manuscript in draft form, and whose learned comments and suggestions have been invaluable.

And finally, I want to thank my family: my parents for my ethical upbringing, and for coping with my challenging and ambitious attitudes during difficult times. My mum's support during my MSc studies, when she took care of my children; my brother Mohammad Baqer, who lent me all his savings when I needed to register for the university entrance exam; my brother Ali Reza, for supporting my business venture through making connections; my sister-in-law Somayyeh, who has done so much to tend for my mum; and my sisters Masumeh and Hakimeh, who looked after my children when I was working in Kabul.

Ibrahim has been my closest friend, always there for me during my good and bad times, and has sacrificed his career for a better life for me and our children; my daughters Sara and Zahra have been so understanding and supporting when times were tough, and have always made us proud; and my little Sina, who miraculously saved my life by his presence.

If you have enjoyed *Shakar*, do please help us spread the word – by putting a review online; by posting something on social media; or in the old-fashioned way by simply telling your friends or family about it.

Book publishing is a very competitive business these days, in a saturated market, and small independent presses such as ourselves are often crowded out by the big houses. Support from readers like you can make all the difference to a book's success.

Many thanks.

Dan Hiscocks
Publisher,
Eye Books

Also published by Eye Books

GOOD MORNING AFGHANISTAN

Waseem Mahmood

It is a time of chaos. Afghanistan has just witnessed the fall of the oppressive Taliban. Warlords battle each other for supremacy, while the powerless, the dispossessed, the hungry and the desperate struggle to survive.

In these days of bleakness, suffering and want, a glimmer of hope emerges – in the form of a spirited little breakfast-time radio programme, Good Morning Afghanistan.

Waseem Mahmood tells how he and an intrepid band of media warriors helped a broken nation find a voice through the radio. Over the airwaves, a land ravaged by decades of war starts to fight with words instead of weapons.

Vividly describes how it feels to be thrown in at the deep end – The Economist

The ideals of hope and humankind's ceaseless quest for freedom shine through in this brilliant work – San Francisco Book Review

A magnificent book – Sacramento Book Review

WHAT ON EARTH CAN GO WRONG

Richard Fenning

After spending three decades advising multinational companies on geopolitics and security crises, Richard Fenning knows all about danger and intrigue. Kidnappings, terrorist attacks, coups d'état, corruption scandals, cyber attacks, earthquakes and hurricanes were all in a day's work in a career that encompassed the rise of China, the tumult of the Middle East wars, the resurgence of populism and the digital revolution.

Amid chaos and upheaval, he also found humanity and humour. Often witty and always insightful, *What on Earth Can Go Wrong* takes us from the battlefields of Iraq to the back streets of Bogotá, from the steamy Niger Delta to the chill of Putin's Moscow.

In a remarkable memoir of a life on the raw edges of globalisation, Fenning looks back with compassion and insight on the people and places he got to know, while offering some timely thoughts on the relationship between risk and fear in a profoundly volatile world.

Beautifully written – a roller-coaster ride of risk – Sir Sherard Cowper-Coles, former British ambassador to Israel and Saudi Arabia

A fascinating insight into the space where politics and business meet, filled with wit and wisdom – Lord Sedwill, former Cabinet Secretary

Take a spoonful of Evelyn Waugh, add a sprinkle of P.J. O'Rourke and garnish with a touch of Michael Palin. Fenning is not just wry, perceptive and informative: he is also laugh-out-loud funny – Boris Starling